THE FRESHWATER FISH COOKBOOK

By Eileen Clarke

Voyageur Press

To Johnny, who really *does* know everything.

Edited by Elizabeth Knight
Series design by Andrea Rud
Printed in Hong Kong

97 98 99 00   5 4 3 2 1

Library of Congress Cataloging-in-Publication Data
Clarke, Eileen.
    The freshwater fish cookbook / by Eileen Clarke.
        p.   cm. — (Fish and game kitchen)
    Includes index.
    ISBN 0-89658-332-5
    1. Cookery (Fish) 2. Freshwater fishes. I. Title. II. Series.
TX747.C62   1996
641.6′92—dc20   96–23137
                                                        CIP

Distributed in Canada by Raincoast Books, 8680 Cambie Street, Vancouver, B.C. V6P 6M9

Published by Voyageur Press, Inc.
123 North Second Street, P.O. Box 338, Stillwater, MN 55082 U.S.A.
612-430-2210, fax 612-430-2211

Please write or call, or stop by, for our free catalog of natural history publications. Our toll-free
number to place an order or to obtain a free catalog is 800-888-WOLF (800-888-9653).

Educators, fundraisers, premium and gift buyers, publicists, and marketing managers:
Looking for creative products and new sales ideas? Voyageur Press books are available at
special discounts when purchased in quantities, and special editions can be created to your
specifications. For details contact the marketing department.

Page 1: *Chilled Barbecued Salmon Steaks with Fennel Salsa*

CONTENTS

Baked Walleye Fillets in Tangerine Sauce

INTRODUCTION

Like most people, I grew up thinking fish was fried shrimp on Friday night, lobster tail on a date, or crab salad sandwich on a hot summer's afternoon. But this is a cookbook for people who catch their own fish, and I don't know too many anglers who tie a shrimpy bugger, lobster muddler, or pale evening dun in crab colors for their tackle box. Most of us live in trout, walleye, and catfish country, and we eat what we catch—finned fish, not shellfish. Which brings us to the crux of the issue: eating our catch.

There's nothing more frustrating than having a freezer full of fish and a family that won't eat it—or will only eat it wrapped in batter and deep fried. We all know those guiltfree days of not watching our fat intake are over. But how do you change your family's tastes? It's a question I asked several years ago. I wanted to eat more fish, but I didn't want to always eat it fried. Cookbooks weren't a whole lot of help; the more I bought and browsed, the more frustrated I got. Shellfish, snapper, sole, and mahi mahi recipes are rampant. Trout, salmon, and catfish may get one recipe each, but perch, walleye, and pike are nowhere to be found. As far as many cookbook authors are concerned, nobody catches these fish.

Well, I'm a nobody with a freezer full of pike, walleye, perch, and salmon, as well as a small creek full of trout a short walk from my kitchen door, and this is a cookbook for people like me. I've got nothing against frying fish; it's a delicious way to cook them. But if I'm starting out with a high-quality, low-fat food, I want a choice of cooking methods. So in these pages, we will deep-fry some fish in batter, and quick-fry others in butter and bread crumbs, but we will also poach, braise, grill, broil, and bake and flake them. Some recipes will be for those who love the taste of fish, uncluttered and unadulterated, but there's also a wide range of choices for those who sort of like fish and think they should eat more, and for those who really can't stand the thought of eating anything but shellfish. We have one each of those first two types of people in our household, and often cook for the third. So open the freezer and dig in. And while you're cooking, remember the warm summer days, the soft spring rains, and those cool fall afternoons with family and friends—memories that are stowed away in those packages along with the catch.

Fishing for trout in Leigh Lake in the Grand Teton National Park (Photo © Erwin and Peggy Bauer)

From Creel to Table

I know of only one disadvantage to eating a truly fresh, wild fish: You have to catch one. You can't buy them in the store, "borrow" one from a friend, or expect someone to drop one off on your porch whenever you feel like it. You have to rig up, suit up, read up, and catch them for yourself.

Most people would also list that as a major advantage to eating truly fresh, wild fish. Like me. I love the solitude of a hot summer's day, wading wet up past my knees in the creek outside my kitchen door. Or stealing one day from elk hunting to fish the brown-trout run, laying tiny flies on the water, and having Moby Fish roll his wide, yellow belly over the line and snap it off.

Right now I'm waiting for that first March afternoon— and there is one every year—when the cold winter sun flicks on the switch. You don't even notice it at first, straining to keep the nymph, or at least the leader, in sight in that cold, gray water. It's what you stop doing that you notice: You stop hunching your shoulders to keep warm and realize your left ear *is* warm, even out there unprotected.

What I like most of all is not having to quarter my fish to get them home, as I do elk and moose. That's definitely on the advantage side of the why-I-eat-wild-fish list.

The list really grows when you get to the kitchen. First of all, since you know when you caught your own fish, you don't need to poke and prod the meat to see how fresh it is. You *know* how fresh it is. You don't need to age it, or marinate it for three days like *sauerbraten* and *hasenpfeffer*. For most fish, cooking is a 10- to 30-minute affair. Fish is tender without doing anything to it.

And there is a wide variety of flavor available to our creels, from the strong, oily taste of salmon to the mild, white flesh of pike and walleye. You can bake it, broil it, fry it. You can cut fillets or steaks, even leave it whole, from a pan-sized brook-trout-on-a-stick to a 30-pound (15-kg) barbecued salmon, for your son's wedding.

And unlike many pursuits, the advantages multiply the more time you spend fishing. The initial investment in waders, rods, reels, and paraphernalia can be written off as mental health care and/or aerobic exercise equipment, or simply prorated per hour of enjoyment, and in a short time, you end up with the allegedly nonexistent free lunch. With a few simple precautions, that free lunch can be delicious whether enjoyed fresh from the stream or served six months later fresh from the freezer.

In the Field

As soon as you catch it, the fish starts going downhill. If you keep three things in mind, you will arrive home with clean, unspoiled fish for cooking.

1. When wading a stream, always carry a creel if you intend to keep fish, and wet the creel down often. On warm days, limit creel time to 3 to 4 hours at most. Ice the fish as soon as possible. If you're on a boat, or fishing near your campsite, ice them immediately. Use chips or cubes rather than blocks: Chips come into closer contact with the fish, cooling them down more quickly and completely, leaving little chance for spoilage.

2. Kill the fish you are keeping immediately, and clean them within 30 minutes of catching, removing the viscera, kidneys—that long red line on either side of the spine—as well as the gills. The gills are full of blood, and fish blood will spoil quickly. Once cleaned, rinse the

fish in clean water, and ice them down.

3. Do not leave live fish on stringers. Delicate fish will bruise themselves fighting the stringer, and warmer water—like bass, pike, and walleye habitat—is a classic breeding ground for bacteria. A dead fish on the stringer is like a chunk of bread in a petri dish: a science experiment you don't want to conduct.

Preparing Fish for the Freezer or Table

The first decision to make is how to prepare your fish, and this depends on what size and type of fish you have to work with. A 6-inch (15-cm) brook trout, while impossible to fillet or steak out, is delicious fried whole in a sea of butter. But what about larger fish? My three rules of thumb are these: First, a panfish is always a panfish, whether it's a trout or a crappie, as long as it fits in a 9-inch (23-cm) frying pan. Second, a steak must be at least 3 inches (7.5 cm) across to be a steak. And third, a fillet can be taken from almost any fish larger than pan size.

Preparation then becomes a matter of taste: Do you eat all your fish in steak form, either fried, broiled or barbecued? Or do you eat it in fish sticks, kabobs, salads, and patties, all of which are easily made from fillets? Since it's faster and easier to fillet two sides than to cut a steak every 1 to 2 inches (2½ to 5 cm), time becomes an important factor. Think of what you order at restaurants, and fill your freezer accordingly.

Filleting Fish

There are two ways to fillet: first is head to tail; second is tail to gills. To begin at the head, lay the cleaned fish on a cutting board and cut straight down through the top fillet to the spine, just behind the gills. Turn the fillet knife parallel to the cutting board and flat to the spine, and, holding the head firmly, run the knife down the spine to the tail. Now lay the this fillet on the cutting board, skin side down. Grasping the tail, slide the knife between flesh and skin at a 20- to 30-degree angle, and slice down the length of the fillet, peeling the flesh off

The end of a good day (Photo © John Barsness)

the skin. A good skinning job will leave no flesh on the hide. Now do the other fillet. Grasp the head to anchor the fish in place for that first cut.

If the head has already been removed while cleaning, it is easier to start to fillet from the tail. Grasp the tail (wrap it in a paper towel to get a good grip), and slide the knife along the tail, parallel to the cutting board and flat against the spine. Angle the knife up at the gills, and remove the fillet. Skin as above.

Cutting Steaks

To cut steaks, lay the cleaned fish on a cutting board. Remove the fins. Using a sharp, heavy knife, cut crosswise (at a 90-degree angle to the spine) through the fish from gills to tail, until the steaks become too small. For quick frying or barbecuing, steaks should be $\frac{3}{4}$–$1\frac{1}{2}$ inches (2–$3\frac{1}{2}$ cm) thick. Any thinner and they will fall apart on the grill; any thicker, and the outside will be scorched before the inside is done.

Leaving Fish Whole

This again is a matter of taste. I know lots of people who clean and keep one lake trout or salmon whole for a summer barbecue party. Then, with the rest of their catch, they fillet a few pieces for smoking, curing, and one-dish meals, and steak the rest.

Panfish can go either way, too. Leave them whole, and you can pick the meat cleanly from the bones after cooking; fillet them, and you're done with the bones before they ever hit the freezer.

Trimming

Filleting generally also includes skinning the fish. Salmon and trout are often left skin-on, both for grilling and curing; white bass and a lot of larger fish—like lake trout—improve in flavor with the fatty skin removed.

Trimming goes one step further. Using a sharp fillet knife, slice all the silver-white membrane and darker fat from the flesh. Then remove the darker flesh along the lateral line.

Fat lends a lot of flavor to fish, both desirable and undesirable. If you like strong-tasting fish, fine. But if you are one of the millions who like more delicate fish, careful trimming will ensure a more delicate flavor. If you don't know where you stand, divide one fillet in two. Cook one half cleaned and scaled, and the other with all skin, fat, and dark flesh removed. Let your taste buds dictate your choice.

Freezing Fish

Fresh is best, but if you like fish, you'll want to keep a few for those days when you can't go out to the lake or stream. Or, if you are lucky enough to have a really productive day on your favorite lake, there's no reason not to freeze the catch. But speed is essential. Think of a freshly caught fish like corn in the garden: Freeze it that day.

Packaging Material

There is a wide choice in packaging, but only two goals: to remove all the air and to have a strong outer layer that won't tear during months in the freezer. Freezer paper, for instance, is sturdy, but on odd-shaped packages like whole fish, a heavy-duty aluminum foil will conform more easily to the shape. The tight-fitting packaging means less chance of trapping air, the main cause of freezer burn. With that in mind, here are some of the most common methods of wrapping fish for storage.

1. For whole fish, wrap the clean fish in waxed paper, then in aluminum foil, folding over and sealing all the outside seams. There's no need for tape, except to label and date the contents.

2. A second method, for long storage, is to fill a large resealable plastic bag with water, add the fish, and carefully work all the bubbles up to the top of the bag. Add more water as needed until about $\frac{1}{2}$-inch (1-cm) headspace is left, then seal the bag, and freeze upright. The ice will provide insulation to protect the fish from freezer burn.

3. For steaks and fillets, wrap individual fillets and steaks in plastic wrap or waxed paper, being careful to press out all the air. Then stack enough individual servings for one family meal, and wrap the stack in heavy-duty aluminum foil.

4. For longer storage, place the fillets in resealable plastic bags, fill the bags with water, and work the air bubbles out the top, leaving adequate headspace for expansion in the freezer. Seal and freeze upright. For really small pieces or small whole fish, fill a milk carton half full with water, then add the fish loosely, cover the fish with water, but leave $\frac{1}{2}$-inch (1-cm) headspace. Close the carton, seal with tape, and freeze upright. Once the plastic bags or milk cartons are frozen, you can stack them any way you want.

The Freezer and Quick-Freezing

Aside from protecting the fish from air, the most important thing is ensuring the fish freezes quickly and stays frozen at a constant 0° Fahrenheit (−17.8° Celsius). To freeze quickly, add only $1\frac{1}{2}$ pounds (750 g) of fish per 1 cubic foot (30 cc) of freezer space at a time, with the freezer temperature set at 0°F (−17.8°C). Stand the packages of fish upright with space between them for the cold to circulate, or lay them flat on freezer shelves. Do not stack piles of room-temperature fish one on top of the other. Hanging baskets are perfect for quick-freezing, so is setting the packages against the sides of the freezer.

Quick-freezing prevents the formation of ice crystals between the fibers of the flesh, which can alter the taste and texture of stored fish. We have two freezers that have the capacity to freeze up to 50 pounds (25 kg) of fish at a time, and have a total space of 30 cubic feet (9 cubic meters), which for us is more than adequate. But if you have more fish than freezer space for quick-freezing, check with your local meat processor on the availability of a quick-freezing unit. It makes a big difference at the table.

With good, solid wrap, your fish will stay fresh 3 to 6 months, especially if you only open the freezer once a week. If all you have is a refrigerator freezer unit, and open it daily, the freezer life of your fish will be quite short. If you want to freeze large quantities over a long time, invest in a chest freezer to maintain proper temperature. Even then, oily fish, such as salmon and lake trout, simply won't keep as well as leaner varieties, such as walleye, perch, and pike. Since the oil is mostly in the skin, you could always skin oily fish before freezing, but still cook them within 3 months.

Thawing Frozen Fish

Never thaw fish on the counter at room temperature—that's another science experiment. If you have time, set the package in the bottom of the refrigerator for 24 hours. If time is short, microwave a 1-pound ($\frac{1}{2}$-kg) package 2 minutes at 500 watts, then 30 seconds at a time, until tiny white spots appear in the thinnest parts of the fish. The thick parts will still be partially frozen; just allow a little more cooking time.

Blue-ribbon trout water: Yellowstone River in Paradise Valley, Montana (Photo © Erwin and Peggy Bauer)

The Smoking Point

No matter where I look for new ways to cook fish, everyone has a recipe for frying. It's the number-one method for most of us. So, a few words about the oil. It doesn't really matter what you use for sautéing or frying at low temperatures, but quick-frying and deep-frying strain oil molecules to the limit. Most oils and shortening are totally inadequate for high-temperature frying; they start smoking long before you are ready to cook. (And if you want to eat fish instead of fat-soaked cardboard, you need to fry at high temperatures.) Unless you're making blackened fish when you want the burned fat to add color to the fish, use peanut, corn, and canola oils. These oils provide that golden brown outside and light, delicate inside that we crave. Strain the cooking oil once in a while, and it will last a long time.

Fish Farms

Finally, a word about fish farms. I recently read an article about catfish in a high-circulation cooking and lifestyle magazine: The quality of farmed catfish, it said, was carefully controlled. When ready for harvest, the fish are transported to the processing plant in tank trucks, processed immediately, and taste-tested. So far so good, but the article didn't stop there. Wild catfish *can be* high quality, they sniffed, but aren't subject to those quality controls—or tank trucks—farmed fish are. They are bottom-feeders and can taste muddy.

It took me a minute to find the list of contributors to this magazine. The list consisted of fish distributors and retailers, with a few university professors thrown in for balance. It made me wonder if any of them had ever tasted wild catfish, which are rarely "muddy" flavored. And what about the softer flesh and cookie-cutter bodies of farmed fish? It's nice that catfish and Atlantic salmon and trout are now available for the nonangler, but they're not "better" food. If you don't believe me, next time you catch a trout, cook it right next to a grocery-store rainbow trout. There's nothing better than a fresh, wild fish.

COOL-WATER AND
WARM-WATER FISH

Northern Pike and Pickerel

Several years ago, there was a small item in the local newspaper about the mysterious disappearance of newly hatched, and swimming, ducklings in a Kalispell, Montana, municipal pond. Kalispell isn't exactly a hotbed of violent crime, so it was puzzling. Then one evening, someone actually saw one of the ducklings get taken.

"It was horrible," the woman cried. "A great monster rose out of the bottom of the lake and devoured that poor little duck."

And thus the centuries-old legend of "Pike, the Monster of the Deep" grew by one duckling. It was a northern pike, probably average size, doing what all of us do: eating lunch. Now, I grant that he would have been smarter to wait for the duck to get bigger, as we do, but pike don't exactly have free access to the meat department at Safeway. They are carnivores, like most other cool-water game fish, and they must eat. But pike are the most notorious, most feared, and most mythic of cold-water flesh-eaters. Isaak Walton in his classic *The Compleat Angler* describes an encounter with a man-eating pike: "His bait was seized by this furious creature, which by a sudden jerk pulled him in, and doubtless would have devoured him also, had he not . . . escaped the dreadful jaws of this voracious animal." Maybe ducklings need to fear pike, but pike need to fear man, because they are, in fact, most delicious to eat.

Northern pike and pickerel are of the same biological family, Esocidae, as well as the same flavor family, Tasty. While there are slight variations in color, fin and scale counts, and markings, the most obvious and useful difference is in size. Pickerel are the smallest, with the record chain pickerel at 9 pounds 6 ounces ($4\frac{1}{4}$ kg), and redfin and grass pickerel are even smaller. The record for pike is 55 pounds 1 ounce ($24\frac{3}{4}$ kg), with 5 to 25 pounds ($2\frac{1}{4}$–$11\frac{1}{4}$ kg) being a more likely catch, depending on the fishing pressure.

As usual there is a direct ratio between total angler poundage and total fish poundage, with pike being consistently more popular than it's cousins. Pickerel are simply too small to be a major attraction to most anglers; muskellunge too rare and hard to catch. The muskie's large size demands an increase in habitat area. Like when hunting elk, you may get into a "herd" of muskie, but you will burn a lot of fuel and eat a lot of baloney sandwiches finding it. Like elk, muskie are considered a trophy except muskie are usually released after one roll of film. Pike are just the right size to provide an enjoyable and profitable day of fishing, and thus attract the most attention from anglers.

All members of the pike family have lean, white, flaky meat, are mild tasting, and, because of their characteristic cigar shape, provide more steaks per pound than a flatter fish. You simply don't need as heavy a pike to cut steaks as you would walleye, bass, or catfish. All pike also have a thick slime coating on their flesh to help them slide through the weeds faster on their way to a tasty duckling. If you want to cook the fish whole, or cook the steaks with skin on, this slimy coating is easily removed by rinsing the whole fish in cold, running water, and then wiping the fish down with a paper towel. Otherwise, simply remove the skin and coating when you fillet. Finicky eaters will likely prefer their pike steaks skinned before cooking; avid fish lovers should leave it on for a richer fish taste. Fillets are almost always skinned.

The pike family also has one more series of bones than walleye and trout. The Y bones run through the meat alongside the spine and cause problems for some cooks, but there are two easy ways to deal with them.

1. For steaks, lay the steak out on a cutting board. At the top center is the spine; enclosing the now-absent viscera is the rib cage. Now imagine a secondary line of ribs located about halfway between the ribs and the outer skin. Those are the Y bones, and they're the only ones that run *through* the meat, and thus, the only ones you need to remove from a steak. Run your fingers along that line and you'll feel them poking through the top of the steak; gently pull the Y bones with a pair of pliers.

2. For fillets, lay the filleted pike out on the cutting board. Imagine cutting the fillet in half lengthwise; then run your fingers down the center of each of those halves, until you feel the sharp tips of the Y. Cut through the fillet on either side of this line of bones to remove them, taking as little flesh as possible. Do the same for each fillet, and you are ready to cook.

Walleye and Perch

The walleye is the largest member of the perch family, and one of the most popular game fish in North America. Native to the northern states and Canada, it has been widely stocked in all but our most extreme climates. Why? It's a combination of being easy to hatch and rear artificially, while also being fun to catch and delicious to eat. Walleye tournaments rival bass tournaments in popularity, and walleye anglers use a lot of the same equipment: big boats, electronic sounding devices, and big coolers full of lunch, pop, and if the angler is lucky, several dozen homemade donuts.

Boone Whitmer of Wolf Point, Montana, is such a lucky man. Farmer, wit, devoted husband and father, he leaves the seeding, planting, and wheat-market research one day a year to go fishing, and only walleye would get him away from his wheat-future listings in July. Such is the lure of this fine-tasting fish.

Walleye live in large lakes, 50 to 100 acres (20–40 hectares) at a bare minimum; they eat other fish, live in schools, and generally feed in dim light. Catch one, and you're likely to have found a bunch and have a great day of fishing. The record walleye is 25 pounds (11¼ kg); average catch 3 to 8 pounds (1¼–3½ kg). If you really want to see how productive a walleye fishery is, go to the local tournament, then hang around for the weigh-in. I did that a few years ago at the Fort Peck, Montana, Governor's Cup, and I almost went out and bought a boat. The "losers" were larger than anything I'd caught in the continental United States, except salmon and lake trout, and were more to my taste in dinner fare.

Walleye are sometimes available in larger fish markets and restaurants, and are highly valued as table fare even by those who don't fish. Your catch will be white-meated, firm, and flaky, with a mild flavor that cooks up into just about anything you want to make. Walleye are also caught in many Canadian lakes, under the names of walleye pike, pike, jack, jackfish, and pickerel. Just be flexible: by commercial and personal standards, the only better-tasting fish is halibut. So fill your freezer, and cook.

Perch have the same flavor and texture of walleye but come in a smaller package, often being more a panfish than the steak and fillet variety. The record for yellow perch is 4 pounds 3 ounces (2 kg), with the standard catch being more in the range of ¼–¾ pound (100–300 g), and in some lakes with optimum conditions, 1–2 pounds (½–1 kg). Despite their small size, perch are one of the major attractions for ice fishermen, and ice-fishing perch tournaments are the highlight of many northern winters. I don't ice fish, but the lure of perch is definitely making me think about taking ice skating lessons. That's how one friend does it: To keep from getting cold and bored, he sets up five holes, 100 yards apart, and ice skates around them.

A caution, however: This winter I was momentarily detained at the fish counter of my grocery store when I saw packages of fish marked "perch fillets." Could they be the real thing? Well, yes. The real *ocean* perch thing, and an entirely different fish.

Bass

The two main species of bass indigenous to North America are smallmouth and largemouth bass. The main difference, aside from the size of their mouths, is habitat: largemouth primarily live in weedy lakes, while their smallmouth siblings hang out in clear, rocky lakes and rivers. Both begin life eating minute crustaceans and graduate to insects, frogs, crayfish, and fish. More importantly, both are fun to catch and great to eat. They take any kind of bait that they think is alive; at 2 inches (5 cm) long, they are already preying on smaller fish. They often jump when hooked; even when not hungry, spawning bass will slash at plugs anyway, out of sheer annoyance.

Bass are all white meat, with a milder flavor than walleye and pike, and medium-firm flesh. They are suitable for filleting, or steaking when large, and are delicious barbecued, grilled, poached, fried, and in the tradition of the Deep South, deep fried. They are also a sunfish, closely related to, but larger than, crappies and bluegills, which is the reason they taste so similar to those fish.

The record for smallmouth bass is 11 pounds 15 ounces (5¼ kg), while the record largemouth is 22 pounds 4 ounces (10 kg). Average size for smallmouth is 1–4 pounds (½–2 kg), while largemouth average 2–6 pounds (1–3 kg). Both have extended their habitat throughout North America through the generosity of local fish and game department stocking efforts, and both are considered a valuable sporting resource.

Catfish

No fish is as closely identified with one region as the catfish is with the Deep South. No South, no catfish; no catfish, no hush puppies. (Tradition says, you must cook the hush puppies in the fat just used to fry the catfish.) But there are more than fifteen families of catfish, indigenous to both North and South America, from walking, talking, and climbing catfish, to the toothless, armored, and blind ones. In our South, we catch channels, blues, marine, flathead, and bullheads. This last, is a miniature catfish often considered a panfish.

Blues are the largest, with the record being 109 pounds 4 ounces (49 kg), while bullheads are at the bottom of the list with an average of less than 1 pound ($\frac{1}{2}$ kg). The record for brown bullheads is a grand 5 pounds 8 ounces ($2\frac{1}{2}$ kg). Flatheads generally weigh 3–4 pounds ($1\frac{1}{2}$–2 kg), but the record is 91 pounds 4 ounces (41 kg). The king of catfish hill, however, the one most popular to catch and cultivate, is the channel cat. Most commonly taken at 11–30 inches ($27\frac{1}{2}$–75 cm) in length and up to 15 pounds ($6\frac{3}{4}$ kg); the record channel is 58 pounds (26 kg). Commercially raised channels are harvested at $1\frac{1}{2}$–5 pounds ($\frac{1}{2}$–$2\frac{1}{4}$ kg), and sold all over the United States, fresh or frozen as whole fish, fillets, steaks, and "nuggets" (I'm not sure what part of a catfish the nugget is). Other cats are also raised commercially, but channels seem to be the cat of choice.

There's a reason catfish are so popular: they have moist, white, flaky flesh with medium-firm texture, and are very lean—3.5 percent fat. The taste is always sweet, whether wild or pond-raised, but the flesh is firmer in wild fish. Wild fish are also a lot more fun to catch, but methods vary wildly, depending on habitat, economic resources, and pure luck. From cheese balls to whole suckers, flies to snag hooks, anglers will do anything to put catfish on the table. Noodling is often a two-angler method, requiring one person to grab the fish by the gills or mouth while both angler and fish are underwater, and the other person to haul them both in. There aren't too many fish that inspire that kind of dedication.

The methods of cooking catfish are legion as well: you can bake, barbecue, broil, braise, poach, and steam them; cook the fish whole, or in fillets, steaks, or those

The results of a good day of fishing for crappie (Photo © Doug Stamm)

mysterious nuggets. But once in your life, deep fry the catfish and then make up a mess of cornmeal hush puppies and fry them in the same oil. Ideally, don't use those commercial, bathtub cats; despite all that applied technology and science, their flesh is not as mild or firm as wild catfish. Wild cats often live in running water, and, even in lakes, swim all their lives, developing muscle tone those tub cats can only dream about. And despite their reputation, their habitat is not limited to the South. Catfish are found as far north as the Great Lakes, and even sub-arctic Montana and Canada—in our slower moving, plains rivers. So check your maps, grab a rod and some bait, or just a friend and a rope, and catch a wild catfish.

Panfish

As much as catfish call up the South, panfish remind me of family. My grandmother introduced me to worm fishing as a toddler, and my toddling son took his first dip in a lake while I was hauling in sunfish. That son gets married this summer, and in the twinkling of an eye, I'll have my own grandchild to introduce to the joys of fishing, and fifty years have gone by. You don't need expensive equipment, you don't need to pay attention, you don't need a blue-ribbon committee to tell you where to fish. If you happen onto a pile of hungry or spawning panfish, you can sometimes even catch them on a bare hook, or hold out a bucket and say please; if you don't, there's a cooler full of hot dogs and marshmallows. You won't go hungry. And no one will get bent out of shape for having the smallest fish. If they do, they need to go back to second grade and learn how to play well with others, or just quit reading Hemingway. Panfish include yellow perch, bluegill, crappie, bullhead, rock bass, pumpkinseed, and any fish—yes, even trout—small enough to fry in a standard-sized frying pan. For the record, that is 8–9 inches (20–23 cm)—no mega-pans allowed. This is strictly a can-you-hold-it-in-the-palm-of-one-hand category. Species is incidental, and all panfish are food; I don't know anyone who practices catch-and-release with bluegill. They are plentiful, easy to cook, and good to eat.

There are two basic ways to prepare panfish for cooking.

1. Simply clean the fish, rinse in clean water, and pat dry with a paper towel. The drying prevents the water from popping in the frying pan, and thus avoids burning the cook with hot oil. You can also remove the head.

2. Clean the fish as in the first method, then lay it out on a cutting board. With a sharp boning knife, angle from just behind the head and gills, down to the vent. In both methods, if you plan to eat the skin, scale the fish.

Is Dinner Ready? Testing for Doneness

The methods for testing whether or not the fish is done are legion, and the easiest way to describe it is to begin with a test. In any pan you wish, boil about one cup of water; then place a piece of fish, any fish, at least one inch square into the boiling water. What was once shiny and translucent—even transparent in some fish—turns white and opaque right before you eyes. Remove the chunk of fish immediately after it turns opaque, and it is moist but done; if you leave it boiling a while, it is still done but getting dry. This is also a good way to determine how you want you fish to be finished. Some people like their fish slightly translucent—what is traditionally still raw (except in poached fish). Others like to take it past the moist-looking stage. Here are several traditional, time-honored ways to test fish so that they are moist, but done.

1. The meat thermometer: For whole fish, the thermometer will read 135°F (57°C) when done. Allow 10 minutes after you've taken the fish out of the oven, for the temperature to reach its peak.

2. The skin: The skin on a properly cooked fish will peel off easily, taking no flesh with it.

3. Texture: The oldest and most commonly used method to test fish for doneness is to test it with a fork. Insert the fork into the thickest part of the fish, usually along the front end of the spine, and gently twist. The flesh should give, not fall apart; and it should be moist-looking rather than dry. While everyone talks about a cooked fish being flaky, an over-cooked fish is also flaky, so measure both.

4. Color: Pale- and white-fleshed fish like walleye and light trout will be opaque but shiny when ready.

Orange-fleshed fish will be paler and less shiny than when raw. Look for the color of the fish when you flake it with a fork. When barbecuing, most fish will fan open when nearly done, and you can check the inside flesh, along the spine, for color. In fact, you can watch the flesh turn from pink to white, thin ribs to thick back as it cooks. Remove the fish as soon as the meat is white throughout, and you will have a moist fish.

Panfish are generally dredged in flour, cornmeal, or crumbled corn flakes, then fried whole with the skin on. If the fish are large enough, you can also fillet each side, skin, and cut the fillet into strips to be dredged in meal and fried. The trick, however, is not to overcook the tender flesh. Use peanut, canola, or any oil with an equally high smoking point, heat it to just below smoking, and fry the fish quickly, until each side is just golden, then remove it from the pan. If you're watching your fat intake, or just want a change, you can also bake the fish at 400°F (205°C) until opaque, and flake the flesh off with your fingers to eat outright or to add to a salad or other dish. When you are camping and there's no oven to use, simply poach the fish in a covered pan, in just enough water, white wine, or extra-dry vermouth to provide moist heat. Then flake as above.

More Delicate Flavor:
The Lateral Line and Fat

We've all seen it: Once you fillet a fish, and skin it, there's a dark line that runs down the middle of the fillet from gill to tail. Part of that is simply fat, but part is the lateral line, essential to the fish and its survival. The lateral line consists of sense organs that not only help the fish maintain its balance in a dim landscape, but also send out signals much like a submarine's sonar system, to locate objects in their immediate vicinity—like food and concrete dams. For some fish, the lateral line is only the beginning of an extensive system of sense organs.

The problem is that the lateral line, and the dark-looking flesh around it—fat—detract from the flavor of the fish. Once again, it's a matter of taste. A lot of people prefer that their fish taste quite definitely like a fish. There are also people who like liver, limburger cheese, and lutefisk. Personally, I like the milder flavor of fish with the lateral line removed.

If you also prefer a milder flavor, or are tasting a particular species of fish for the first time and aren't sure what to expect, lay the skinned fillet on a cutting board, and with a thin, sharp fillet knife, slice out the darker areas of the lateral line and the fat. I recently did a test on two white bass fillets: On one I removed the lateral line and surface fat, on the other I left them in. The taste difference was dramatic. With all fat and nerve tissue removed, the white bass had a delicate and mild taste, which I prefer. My husband John enjoyed the untrimmed fillet, but admitted that, given a choice, he would always remove them. Experiment with your family; many cool- and warm-water fish benefit from careful trimming.

Flexible Fish for the Cook

The puzzling part for me has always been that no matter what they eat, cool- and warm-water fish have the same pale, mild-tasting flesh. That's not true with most other species. Remember those ducklings? If I go up to Alberta, Canada, to hunt those ducks as adults, and am lucky enough to put a few grain-fed mallards in my bag, they taste wonderful. A month later, those same ducks will come flying off those Canadian wheatfields, and sit on the November Montana lakes, feeding on the frozen, and by now decaying, underwater vegetation. That slimy feed makes a January mallard taste worlds different from the wheat-fed bird.

But cool- and warm-water fish can eat anything from bugs to toads; they can live in lakes or rivers, close to the surface, down on the bottom, or slithering through the weeds, in muddy or crystal clear water. It simply doesn't matter. They always taste like fish—like the pike, bass, or walleye you caught 500 miles, two years, or two seasons past. And while the recipes in this section of the book are designed and labeled for each individual type of fish, if you have a freezer full of walleye, there's no reason why you should limit yourself to the "walleye" recipes only. The size of the fish and the tastes of your family should be the only things that determine if you should use a bass recipe on a pike, or pike recipe on walleye. Large fish tend to have increased oil content, and are much better for smoking than smaller fish, but are less tasty for fried dishes. But otherwise, when it comes to cool- and warm-water fish, a steak recipe is a steak recipe and a fillet is a fillet. Mix, mingle, experiment: Don't ever get bored with a freezer full of delicious wild fish.

Lake fishing (Photo © John Barsness)

SWEET AND SOUR FISH BITS

Yield: 4 servings

Fish Bits makes a wonderful appetizer, or served with rice, a main dish with a Chinese flavor. Make them with pike, walleye, bass, or any other mild-flavored fish fillets you have in your freezer. But make lots—the bits go down fast.

Sweet and Sour Fish Bits

Ingredients
1 pound (½ kg) fillets, cut into chunks
2 egg whites
2 tablespoons corn starch
4 green onions, chopped
1 teaspoon ground ginger
Vegetable oil for frying
4 tablespoons sugar
2 tablespoons sake (Japanese rice wine) or
    extra-dry vermouth
2 tablespoons soy sauce
2 tablespoons rice vinegar
2 teaspoons corn starch
2 tablespoons water

Cooking
1. Cut up the fish in 1–2 inch (2½–5 cm) chunks, and pat dry with a paper towel. In a small bowl, combine the egg whites and the 2 tablespoons corn starch. Stir well to get all the lumps out. Add the fish bits to the corn starch mixture and toss to coat.

2. In a large skillet over medium heat, add the green onions and ginger to 1 tablespoon of cooking oil and stir about 1 minute. Add the sugar, sake, soy sauce, and vinegar, and stir until the sugar dissolves. Remove the sauce from the heat.

3. In a deep fat fryer, or skillet with oil to cover, fry the corn starch-coated bits a few at a time until lightly golden. Drain on paper towels.

4. When all the fish are fried, reheat the sauce over medium heat, and add the fish. Stir to coat. Dissolve the 2 teaspoons corn starch in the water and add to the pan. Cook until thickened, stirring constantly. Serve hot as an appetizer or as main dish with rice.

PIKE RAVIOLI IN MARINARA SAUCE

Yield: Four dozen ravioli

Sometimes it's worth doing things the hard way, like ravioli. If you've never tasted anything but canned or frozen ravioli, you owe it to yourself to try this. This recipe uses a food processor to mix the dough, a rolling pin to stretch it out, and an inexpensive two-piece form to assemble the ravioli. If you have a pasta maker, that makes it even easier. And there are shortcuts. If you don't have the time, buy yourself a package of 50 wonton skins, and a crimping tool; you'll have custom-made ravioli in 30 minutes. It's still better than what you get in the can.

Ingredients

2 teaspoons dried leaf marjoram
1 teaspoon salt
1 teaspoon pepper
2 teaspoons onion powder
1 pound ($\frac{1}{2}$ kg) cooked pike fillets or scraps
2 eggs
3 tablespoons water
2 cups (500 ml) sifted flour
4 cloves garlic, minced
1 tablespoon oil
1 can whole tomatoes, 28 ounces (795 g)
$\frac{1}{4}$ cup (60 ml) grated Parmesan cheese

Cooking

1. Combine marjoram, salt, pepper, and onion powder. Roll the cooked fish in the mixture and set aside.

2. To make the dough, put the eggs and 1 tablespoon of water into a food processor. Process on high with a metal blade for 2–3 seconds. Now add the flour and continue to process on high, while slowly adding the water 1 tablespoon at a time until the dough forms into a ball. The dough should be slightly sticky and moist, but not dripping.

3. Place the ball on a floured board or counter and knead 1 minute. Then divide into six pieces and lay five aside under a damp cloth. With a rolling pin, roll the first ball out very thin—almost paper thin—into a long rectangle that will overlap your ravioli press. Lay one sheet of dough on the press, and spoon filling into the centers. Moisten the rest of the bottom sheet around the filling, then cover with a top sheet of dough, press, and set aside on a sheet of wax paper. Repeat until all the dough is gone.

4. Now make the sauce (or use a prepared Marinara sauce). In a medium skillet, sauté the garlic in the oil until golden, then add the tomatoes with liquid, and simmer uncovered about 20 minutes until most of the thin liquid has cooked down.

5. While the sauce simmers, start a large pot of water boiling. Add the ravioli to it, about two dozen at a time, cooking about 5 minutes until *al dente*. (The ravioli should not be crowded in the pot.) Top the ravioli with the sauce and Parmesan cheese, and serve with garlic bread, fresh salad, and chocolate pudding—that's what my mom always gave us for dessert after a ravioli dinner.

Lemon Rolled Pike Fillets

Yield: 4 servings

Here's an old classic—lemon and fish—with a slightly different look. It's still easy to fix, and tastes delicious.

Ingredients

1 ½ pounds (¾ kg) thin pike fillets
3 tablespoons butter or margarine
½ teaspoon curry powder
¼ cup (60 ml) diced celery
¼ cup (60 ml) diced green pepper
¼ cup (60 ml) diced onion
1 ¼ cups (300 ml) dried bread crumbs
1 teaspoon shredded lemon peel
¼ cup (60 ml) fresh lemon juice (about 1 lemon)
¼ teaspoon salt
¼ teaspoon pepper
¼ cup (60 ml) minced fresh parsley

Cooking

1. Pat the fillets dry with paper towels. Cut them into four equal pieces, each about 8 inches (20 cm) long. Set aside.

2. In a large skillet, melt 1 tablespoon of the butter over medium heat and add the curry powder. Sauté the celery, green pepper, and onion in this mixture until the vegetables are tender. Remove from the heat, add the bread crumbs and lemon peel, and toss. Combine the lemon juice, salt, and pepper, and stir into the bread-crumb mixture.

3. Preheat the oven to 350°F (175°C). In a lightly greased baking dish, lay out the fillets. Spoon about a quarter of the stuffing over each piece, wrap the fish around the filling, and secure with a toothpick. Melt the other 2 tablespoons of butter, add the parsley, and brush about half of this mixture over the top of the pike rolls.

4. Bake uncovered about 30 minutes, until the fish flakes easily when you gently twist a fork into the thickest part, but it still looks moist. Brush with the rest of the parsley butter before serving. Serve with rice and carrots.

Northern pike (Photo © Doug Stamm)

Pike Kabobs with Peanut Barbecue Sauce

Yield: 4 servings

Members of the pike family—muskie and pickerel included—have firmer flesh than most freshwater fish. That makes kabobs possible. It's not like sticking a piece of red meat on the skewer, but if you thread the fish onto two parallel wooden skewers and handle the works with a bit of care, they have one advantage over red meat: it only takes about 5 minutes to cook a pike kabob.

Pike Kabobs with Peanut Barbecue Sauce

Ingredients

¼ cup (60 ml) fresh lemon juice (about 1 lemon)
¼ cup (60 ml) creamy peanut butter
1 tablespoon Worcestershire sauce
2 tablespoons sugar
⅛ teaspoon curry powder
1 pound (½ kg) pike chunks, 1 inch (2½ cm) thick, 2 inches (5 cm) long

Cooking

1. Combine the lemon juice, peanut butter, and Worcestershire sauce in a saucepan or glass bowl and liquefy on the stove or in the microwave. Add the sugar and curry powder, mix well, and set the sauce aside.

2. The pike chunks can be taken from fillets or steaks, but they must be at least 1 inch (2½ cm) thick. Cut into 2-inch (5-cm) lengths, and thread two wooden skewers through the fish, with the skewers set at least ½ inch (1 cm) apart. You don't even have to soak the skewers first: the fish will be cooked before the wood catches fire.

3. Preheat a propane barbecue or start four dozen charcoal briquettes. Start cooking on the briquettes when they're white hot; once preheated, turn the propane unit down to medium high. Brush the sauce on the fish before putting the kabobs on the grill, then cook, turning and basting twice, about 5 minutes total. Serve with more sauce and a tart tabbouli salad.

Marinated and Broiled Pike Steaks

Yield: 4 servings

A summer's night, a lunker pike, a barbecue, and thou. Pretty romantic. The marinade only takes 3 hours, and the steaks 10 minutes on the grill. What more do you want for summer?

Ingredients

¼ cup (60 ml) oil (but not olive oil)

3 tablespoons rice wine vinegar

1 clove garlic

¼ teaspoon pepper

1 teaspoon dried sweet basil

2 tablespoons chopped fresh parsley

1 tablespoon grated Parmesan cheese

1 pound (½ kg) pike steaks, 1½ inch (4 cm) thick

Cooking

1. Combine all the ingredients except the steaks in a blender and purée. Pour into a resealable plastic bag, then carefully add the pike steaks. Let sit in the refrigerator for 3 hours.

2. Drain the marinade off the steaks and reserve the liquid. Preheat the propane barbecue 5–10 minutes, or start four dozen charcoal briquettes. When the briquettes are white hot or the propane unit turned down to medium high, start the steaks. Cook 10–12 minutes total, turning carefully two or three times, and basting with the reserved marinade each time you turn the steaks.

Northern pike (Photo © Doug Stamm)

PIKE MOUSSE

Yield: 4 servings

Pike Mousse is one of those perfect dishes for the dog days of summer. Use leftovers, or cook up the pike fillets in the microwave for 1 minute or less. The rest is easy, with no cooking required. Who says mousse always has to be salmon?

Ingredients

1 pound (½ kg) pike fillet
½ cup (125 ml) boiling-hot extra-dry vermouth (dry white wine or water will do)
2 tablespoons fresh lemon juice (1/2 lemon)
1 teaspoon grated lemon rind
2 shallots
1 envelope unflavored gelatin
½ cup (125 ml) mayonnaise
1 teaspoon dried dill weed
½ teaspoon dried mustard
1 cup (250 ml) whipping cream.

Cooking

Pike Mousse

1. Dice the fillet, and cook 1 minute in a 500-watt microwave, 30–40 seconds in a 700-watt unit. Let cool to room temperature before using.

2. In a food processor or blender, combine the vermouth, lemon juice, lemon rind, shallots, and gelatin. Purée until the shallots are minced. Add the mayonnaise, dill, mustard, and cooked pike, and purée again for 1 minute. Whip the cream in a separate bowl until fluffy, then add the whipped cream to the blender, a quarter at a time, and blend after each addition.

3. Rinse a 4-cup (1-liter) mold with cold water. Pour in the mousse, cover, and refrigerate overnight. Unmold by dipping mold in hot water for 2–4 seconds, and inverting on a serving dish. Serve with a fresh garden salad and sourdough bread.

QUICK-FRIED PIKE STEAKS WITH TANGY ONION SAUCE

Yield: 4 servings

If you like sweet-and-sour foods as much as I do, you'll love this Tangy Onion Sauce. The good news is, if you start the steaks about the time you turn the sauce down to thicken, it only takes about 15 minutes to cook.

Quick-Fried Pike Steaks with Tangy Onion Sauce

Ingredients

2 tablespoons margarine or butter
2 medium red onions, sliced thin
$\frac{2}{3}$ cup (160 ml) red wine vinegar
6 tablespoons sugar
$\frac{1}{4}$ teaspoon pepper
1 pound ($\frac{1}{2}$ kg) pike steaks, 1 inch (2 $\frac{1}{2}$ cm) thick
2 tablespoons peanut oil

Cooking

1. Tangy Onion Sauce: In a medium-sized skillet over medium heat, melt the butter and sauté the red onions until softened. Add the vinegar, sugar, and pepper to the onions and stir, cooking over medium heat until the onions are glazed and the sauce is thickened.

2. Meanwhile, dry the steaks with paper towels while you heat the peanut oil to the smoking point in a 9-inch (22-cm) skillet. Immediately add the steaks, sear on both sides, then turn the heat down to medium, and continue cooking about 5 minutes total until the fish flakes away easily with a fork. Divide the Tangy Onion Sauce among the steaks and serve.

Stuffed Pike Fillets

Yield: 4–6 servings

These stuffed fillets prove you don't need a whole fish to have stuffing, and the stuffing makes the fish moist and tasty. This is an easy Sunday supper that pleases everyone, even the cook.

Northern pike (Photo © Wally Eberhart —Photo/Nats)

½ cup (125 ml) chopped celery
⅓ cup (80 ml) finely chopped onion
2 tablespoons butter or margarine
1 cup (250 ml) dried bread cubes
1 teaspoon orange zest
1 orange, peeled and diced
¼ cup (60 ml) orange juice
1 tablespoon minced fresh parsley
4 large pike fillets, 8 ounces (200 g) each
¼ teaspoon salt
¼ teaspoon pepper

Cooking

1. In a medium-sized skillet over medium heat, sauté the celery and onion in 1 tablespoon of the margarine until soft. Add the bread cubes, zest, orange pieces, and juice. Toss and continue to sauté until all the liquid is absorbed. Remove from heat and add the minced parsley.
2. Preheat the oven to 350°F (175°C). In a greased 9x13-inch (22x32-cm) baking dish, lay out two of the fillets. Season with half of the salt and pepper, then cover each fillet with half of the stuffing. Top each with one remaining fillet. Melt the second tablespoon of margarine, and brush the top of the fillets. Season with the rest of the salt and pepper, and bake uncovered for 30 minutes. Test by inserting a fork and twisting; the fish should look moist, but flake easily.

Spicy Pike Stew

Yield: 6 servings

Since fish cooks quickly, making stew isn't the all-day affair that red meat requires. This spicy pike stew takes less than 30 minutes from start to finish, and gives the hot-sauce lovers in the family something to cheer about.

Spicy Pike Stew

Ingredients

1–2 teaspoons curry powder
1 teaspoon cumin seeds
½ teaspoon ground cardamom
½ teaspoon ground turmeric
¼ teaspoon cayenne pepper
1½ tablespoons oil
1 medium onion, chopped
2 cloves garlic, minced
1 teaspoon freshly grated ginger
½ cup (125 ml) raw wild rice
½ cup (125 ml) raw white rice
1 medium red potato, diced

½ cup (125 ml) clam juice
3½ cups (875 ml) water
½ teaspoon salt
1 cup (250 ml) thawed and chopped frozen spinach
1 pound (½ kg) pike, cut into bite-sized chunks
¾ cup (185 ml) chopped fresh cilantro
¼ cup (60 ml) chopped fresh mint
1 tablespoon butter
1½ cups (375 ml) diced ripe tomato

Cooking

1. In a 5-quart (4¾-liter) Dutch oven or heavy-bottom saucepan over medium-low heat, sauté the curry powder, cumin, cardamom, turmeric, and cayenne pepper in the oil until hot, about 2–3 minutes. Add the onion, garlic, and ginger, and continue cooking until the onion is soft. Add the wild and white rice and stir until the rice is well coated, then add the potatoes, clam juice, water, and salt. Bring the mixture to a boil, reduce the heat to a simmer, cover, and cook 15 minutes.

2. Add the spinach and pike, and continue cooking for 5 minutes. Add the cilantro, mint, butter, and tomato, stir well and serve immediately.

NEW ENGLAND PIKE CHOWDER

Yield: 4–6 servings

New England Pike Chowder

I grew up on both creamy New England and tomato-based Manhattan clam chowders, and I find that freshwater fish is just as good as clams for this traditional soup. Pike holds up well in chowder, but any kind of fish will work. The thought of having a bit of catfish, for instance, or largemouth bass swimming around in New England waters strikes me as a chowder with an attitude.

Ingredients

1 slice of bacon, diced
1 medium onion, finely diced
2 stalks celery, diced
1 teaspoon dried leaf summer savory
2 bay leaves
¼ cup (60 ml) bottled clam juice
2 cups (500 ml) water
3 medium potatoes, diced
1 cup (250 ml) frozen corn, thawed
½ teaspoon salt
½ teaspoon pepper
1 pound (½ kg) pike, diced
½ cup (125 ml) table cream, or ¼ cup (60 ml)
   whipping cream plus ¼ cup (60 ml)
   1 percent milk

Cooking

1. In a heavy-bottomed soup pot or 5-quart (4¾-liter) Dutch oven, brown the bacon over medium heat. Add the onions and celery to the fat and sauté until tender. Add the savory, bay leaves, clam juice, water, potatoes, corn, salt, and pepper, and bring the mixture to a boil. Lower to a simmer, cover, and cook 40 minutes or until the potatoes are tender.

2. Add the fish and cream, stir well to blend the cream, and serve immediately. The fish will cook in less time than it takes to get a spoon and a bowl. Serve with crackers.

PIKE MUDDLE

Yield: 6 servings

A muddle is a classic Carolina-coast fish soup which can include about anything but the kitchen sink. The word "muddle" apparently comes from the original white settlers and means "a pile of fish." In other words, this is a suggestion, not a recipe, so put any white-meated fish in the pot, but don't forget a little shellfish to sweeten it.

Ingredients

4 slices of bacon, cut into 2 inch (5 cm) pieces
2 large yellow onions, coarsely chopped
3 stalks celery, chopped
4 cloves garlic, minced
1 orange rind, grated
1 can whole tomatoes, 28 ounces (795 g)
6 medium potatoes, cubed
4 cups (1 liter) fish stock (see page 74)
1 teaspoon dried leaf thyme
2 teaspoons dried leaf oregano
$\frac{1}{4}$ teaspoon red pepper flakes, or to taste
$\frac{1}{2}$ teaspoon salt
1 pound ($\frac{1}{2}$ kg) fish fillets
$\frac{1}{4}$ pound (100 g) shrimp, shelled and deveined
$\frac{1}{4}$ pound (100 g) scallops
$\frac{1}{2}$ cup (125 ml) chopped green onions
1 tablespoon chopped fresh parsley

Cooking

1. In a large soup pot or 5-quart ($4\frac{3}{4}$-liter) Dutch oven over medium heat, cook the bacon until crisp. Remove the bacon pieces and save on paper towels. In the pan drippings, sauté the onions, celery, garlic, and 1 teaspoon of the orange rind until soft, stirring often. Add the tomatoes and their liquid, the potatoes, fish stock, thyme, oregano, pepper flakes, and salt. Bring to a boil, then reduce the heat to a simmer, and cook covered for about 20 minutes or until the potatoes are tender. To serve later, refrigerate the soup and complete step 2 before serving.

2. Just before serving, bring the soup to a simmer, add the fish, shrimp, and scallops, and cook about 1 minute until the fish is opaque. Combine the rest of the orange rind, green onions, and parsley in a small bowl. To serve, pour the soup into bowls and top with the parsley mixture.

PIKE AU GRATIN

Yield: 4 servings

This is a dish for a special occasion, or just when you need a little cheering up. Buy a small amount of shrimp, fresh or canned, and pull a chunk of pike out of the freezer. Pike au Gratin is easy, and ready in two quick steps.

Ingredients

1 pound ($\frac{1}{2}$ kg) pike fillets
$\frac{1}{2}$ teaspoon salt
$\frac{1}{2}$ teaspoon pepper
1 lemon
3 tablespoons butter or margarine
3 tablespoons white flour
1 cup (250 ml) milk
$\frac{1}{2}$ cup (125 ml) raw or canned shrimp
1 cup (250 ml) Italian-flavored bread crumbs
$\frac{1}{4}$ cup (60 ml) grated Parmesan cheese

Cooking

1. Preheat the oven to 350°F (175°C). In a 2-quart (1$\frac{1}{2}$-liter) baking dish, lay the fillets out in a single layer, season with salt and pepper, and squeeze the juice of 1 lemon over the top. Cover and bake 12 minutes. Remove from the oven and set aside.
2. While the fillets are baking, make the sauce. In a medium-sized saucepan, melt the butter over medium heat, then add the flour. Stir constantly, cooking until the mixture is smooth. Turn the heat down if it gets above a slow bubble. Now add the milk, slowly but steadily, and continue stirring until the sauce thickens up again, about 5 minutes. Add the shrimp and remove from the heat.
3. Preheat the broiler, setting the rack 4–5 inches (10–12$\frac{1}{2}$ cm) from the heat source. Drain the excess liquid off the pike, then sprinkle the bread crumbs over the top of the fillets. Pour the sauce over the bread crumbs and top with the Parmesan cheese. Place under the broiler for about 3 minutes, or until the top is golden brown. Serve immediately.

Note: Use prepared Italian-flavored bread crumbs or follow this recipe: Dry 4 slices of white bread in a warm oven for about 1–2 hours. Break the bread slices into crumbs, and place the crumbs, 1 teaspoon sweet basil, $\frac{1}{2}$ teaspoon rosemary, $\frac{1}{4}$ teaspoon ground sage, $\frac{1}{4}$ teaspoon garlic powder, and 1 teaspoon onion powder in a food processor or blender, and blend, on high for 10 seconds. Makes 1 cup (250 ml) of flavored bread crumbs.

BROILED PIKE FILLETS WITH LEMON-CHIVE SAUCE

Yield: 4 servings

The problem with wild fish fillets is that they aren't cut out with a cookie cutter: they have thick places and thin places on the same fillet. There are two things you can do to remedy this: First, cut the fillets out of the thickest part, then save the thin strips for other meals. Second, cut the individual servings from areas of the same thickness, and then start cooking the thick fillets first and add the thinner ones later. The 1-inch-thick (2½-cm) cuts will take the traditional 10 minutes; thinner strips may take only 3 minutes. Thin pieces don't need to be turned, so be sure the broiler pan is preheated along with the broiler.

Fishing along the Yellowstone River (Photo © Michael Goodman— Photo/Nats)

Ingredients

2 pounds (1 kg) fillets, 1 inch (2½ cm) thick

½ cup (125 ml) melted butter

½ teaspoon salt

¼ teaspoon pepper

2 tablespoons fresh lemon juice

¼ cup (60 ml) chopped chives

Cooking

1. Preheat the broiler. Pat the fillets dry with paper towels. Cut into individual servings and set aside. Cut a length of foil long enough to provide a handle on both ends. Lightly oil the foil, and lay the fillets on top. You can lightly oil a pre-heated broiler rack as well, if you don't want to use foil. The coating keeps the fish from sticking.

2. Combine the butter, salt, pepper, lemon juice, and chives and baste the fish liberally with the sauce. Broil about 3 inches (7 cm) from the heat, 10 minutes per inch of maximum thickness. If the fillets are 1 inch (2½ cm) thick, carefully turn them with a spatula halfway through the cooking, and baste them again (whether you turned them or not).

3. Transfer the cooked fillets to a warmed platter, baste with the rest of the lemon-chive sauce, and serve with wedges of lime.

FROZEN PIKE FILLETS WITH HERBED BUTTER

Yield: 4 servings

So you forgot to take something out of the freezer for dinner? Don't worry, use frozen fish. Instead of taking 10 minutes to cook that 1-inch-thick (2½-cm) fillet, allow 20 minutes for fish that's frozen solid. And don't worry about the fish suffering from the ordeal. You might find you like it better.

Ingredients

6 tablespoons butter or margarine, softened
2 cloves garlic, minced
1 teaspoon dried leaf oregano
½ teaspoon salt
½ teaspoon pepper
1 tablespoon freshly squeezed lime juice
1½ pounds (¾ kg) frozen pike fillets, 1 inch (2½ cm) thick

Cooking

1. Preheat the broiler and broiler rack. Combine all of the ingredients except the fish in a small bowl and stir well. Lightly oil a length of foil and arrange the fillets on top. Brush the fillets with the butter mixture.

2. Broil the fillets 4 inches (10 cm) from the heat, about 8 minutes to a side. Turn carefully with a long spatula halfway through the cooking, and test for doneness after the second 8 minutes. Gently insert a fork into the thickest part, and twist: the fish is done when the meat flakes, but still looks moist. Even though you start out with frozen fish, it's still possible to overcook, so check carefully.

MARINATED PIKE FILLETS

Yield: 2–3 servings

The semi-firm flesh of pike and walleye are perfect for marinating. The marinade gives them flavor, and the oil keeps the meat moist while cooking.

Ingredients

½ cup (125 ml) olive oil
2 tablespoons balsamic vinegar
¼ teaspoon salt
¼ teaspoon pepper
1 tablespoon dried leaf oregano
1 tablespoon dried leaf thyme
1 pound (½ kg) walleye or pike fillet, 1 inch (2½ cm) thick

Cooking

1. Combine the oil and vinegar, whisk well, and add the seasonings. Place the fish in a shallow glass or plastic dish and pour the marinade over the top. Marinate 15–30 minutes in the refrigerator, turning the fillet several times.

2. Preheat the broiler and broiler pan. Once the broiler is ready, remove the broiler pan, and brush it lightly with oil. Remove the fish from the marinade, draining the excess liquid back into the bowl. Place the fillet on the oiled broiler pan and broil about 3 inches (7½ cm) from the heat, basting occasionally with the remaining marinade. Broil a 1-inch (2½-cm) fillet 8–10 minutes. Thinner fillets take as little as half the time. Test for doneness by inserting a fork into the thickest part and gently twisting. The fish is done when the meat is opaque but still moist, and the flesh flakes easily.

PIKE IN WINE SAUCE

Yield: 4 servings

You don't need pike for this flavorful wine sauce; any member of the Y-bone family will do, as will walleye and perch if the fillet is thick enough to broil. Sake—Japanese rice wine—can be substituted for vermouth.

Fishing at sunset (Photo © Doug Stamm)

Ingredients

1 pound (½ kg) pike fillet, 1 inch (2½ cm) thick
½ teaspoon salt
¾ teaspoon pepper
¼ cup (60 ml) butter or margarine
3 cloves garlic, finely minced
1 cup (250 ml) extra-dry vermouth
¼ cup (60 ml) minced fresh parsley
4 drops red pepper Tabasco sauce

Cooking

1. Pat the fillets dry with a paper towel, and cut into individual servings. Season with half of the salt and pepper, and set aside. Preheat the oven to 350°F (175°C).
2. Melt the butter in a small saucepan. Add the garlic, vermouth, parsley, Tabasco sauce, and the rest of the salt and pepper.
3. Place the fillet in a lightly oiled baking pan, pour the sauce over the fillet, and bake 6–8 minutes. Test by sticking a fork in the thickest part of the fillet and gently twisting. The fish is done when it is moist, but flakes easily. Serve as an appetizer with a wedge of lemon, or as a main dish with risotto and fresh salad.

PICKEREL ALFREDO

Yield: 4 servings

Here's the classic Italian cream-and-pasta dish with that good old American pickerel—a delicious meal ready in minutes. Next time you go camping, you can trade in that old box of Rice-a-Roni for a dish of real food.

Ingredients

8 ounces (200 g) fettucine or thin spaghetti

4 tablespoons butter or margarine, melted

1 cup (250 ml) whipping cream, at room temperature

$\frac{3}{4}$ cup (185 ml) grated Parmesan cheese

4 ounces (100 g) pickerel meat, cooked and flaked

2 ounces (50 g) prosciutto, cut into thin strips

$\frac{1}{2}$ teaspoon salt

$\frac{1}{2}$ teaspoon pepper

Cooking

1. Cook the fettucine as directed on the package, drain, and transfer to a large, warmed bowl.

2. Add the remaining ingredients quickly, toss to coat all the pasta, and serve at once.

Lake fishing (Photo © Doug Stamm)

PICKEREL AND SEAFOOD ENCHILADAS

Yield: 4 large enchiladas

Sometimes cheating is delicious: in this case, we're adding a little bit of ocean-going shellfish to a delicate-tasting lake fish and making enormous, delicious enchiladas. This recipe is perfect for all those people who say they hate fish.

Ingredients

1 can diced tomatoes, 28 ounces (795 g)
$\frac{2}{3}$ cup (160 ml) chopped onion
2 cloves garlic
$\frac{1}{2}$ cup (125 ml) loosely packed, fresh cilantro
$\frac{1}{2}$ teaspoon salt
6 tablespoons butter
4 teaspoons ground coriander
4 teaspoons green Jalapeño Tabasco sauce
8 ounces (200 g) scallops
8 ounces (200 g) shrimp
1 pound ($\frac{1}{2}$ kg) pickerel pieces
4 flour tortillas, 12 inches (30 cm) in diameter
8 ounces (200 g) Monterey Jack cheese, grated

Cooking

1. In a food processor or blender, combine the tomatoes, onion, garlic, cilantro, and salt. Chop 5–7 seconds until almost liquid. Pour into a medium-sized saucepan over low heat and keep warm while you prepare the rest of the dish.

2. Preheat the oven to 450°F (245°C). Melt the butter in a large skillet, add the coriander and green sauce, and stir. Sauté the scallops, shrimp, and pickerel pieces in this mixture until the fish is opaque, about 2–3 minutes.

3. Dip each tortilla in the tomato-cilantro sauce, then spread a quarter of the sautéed fish across the tortilla. Roll the tortilla to close and top with cheese. Bake in the oven for 10 minutes, until the cheese is melted.

PICKEREL PEPPER POT

Yield: 6 servings

Mildly spicy and densely flavored, the pepper pot transforms a delicate, mild-mannered fish into a super dinner. Add more pepper and ginger at your peril.

Ingredients

2 large sweet onions, finely chopped
4 tablespoons margarine or butter
$\frac{1}{4}$ teaspoon cayenne pepper
1 teaspoon sweet paprika
$\frac{1}{4}$ teaspoon black pepper
$\frac{1}{4}$ teaspoon ground ginger
2 cups (500 ml) water
2 pounds (1 kg) pickerel pieces
$\frac{1}{4}$ cup (60 ml) fresh lemon juice (about 1 lemon)

Cooking

1. In a dry 5-quart ($4\frac{3}{4}$-liter) Dutch oven or heavy-bottomed pot over medium heat, brown the onions. Add the butter, and once it has melted, add the cayenne pepper, paprika, black pepper, and ginger. Stir to coat the onions with the spices. Add 1 cup (250 ml) of the water and continue cooking the onions on a low simmer for about 30 minutes.

2. Meanwhile, shred or dice the pickerel, and soak it in lemon juice mixed with the second cup (250 ml) of water or enough water to cover. Let stand 10 minutes, drain the fish, and add it to the onion mixture (which has now been cooking for 30 minutes), stirring it in thoroughly. Cover and simmer about 5 more minutes, until the fish is cooked. Serve over couscous or rice.

CAJUN WALLEYE SALAD

Yield: 4 servings

Two of my favorite restaurants serve a seafood salad that would knock your socks off. But one restaurant is forty-five miles away, the other sixty-five miles. Eventually, I started making my own "seafood" salad, made of my own fresh, freshwater fish. It still knocks your socks off.

Ingredients

2 slices of bacon

¾ cup (185 ml) chopped celery

⅓ cup (80 ml) chopped green pepper

⅓ cup (80 ml) chopped yellow bell pepper

⅓ cup (80 ml) chopped green onions

3 tablespoons frozen orange juice concentrate, thawed

3 tablespoons lime juice

¼ teaspoon powdered Colman's English mustard, or standard dry mustard

Pinch of red pepper flakes

1 can black-eyed peas, 15 ounces (425 g), drained and rinsed

2 very ripe roma or plum tomatoes, diced

1 teaspoon chopped pepperoncini peppers

1½ pounds (¾ kg) walleye fillet, cut into chunks

1½ teaspoons Cajun Shake (recipe follows)

1 teaspoon oil

½ head lettuce

Cooking

1. In a large skillet over medium heat, cook the bacon until crisp. Remove the bacon, crumble, and set aside. Sauté the celery, peppers, and onions in the bacon fat for 1 minute. Set aside.

2. In a large bowl, combine the orange juice concentrate, lime juice, mustard, and red pepper flakes. Mix well, then stir in the celery, mixture. Add the black-eyed peas, tomato, and pepperoncini pepper. Toss gently, cover, and chill at least 1 hour.

3. Put the fish chunks in a large bowl, sprinkle with the Cajun Shake mix, then stir the fish gently to coat it completely.

4. Heat the oil in a large skillet over high heat, add the fish chunks, and sauté about 2 minutes until the walleye chunks are opaque all the way through. Transfer to a bowl, cover, and chill at least 1 hour.

5. To serve, divide the lettuce among four plates, top with a quarter of the pea mixture, then a quarter of the walleye chunks. Top with the crumbled bacon.

CAJUN SHAKE

Yield: ¼ cup (60 ml)

Over the years I've found that most commercially prepared Cajun spice mixes are way too hot for me, and if I use less than they recommend, I lose all the flavor. I solved the problem by making up my own Cajun spice mix. It's full of flavor, but takes a moderate approach to the pepper half of the Cajun tradition.

Ingredients

2 ½ tablespoons sweet paprika
1 tablespoon garlic powder
1 tablespoon onion powder
1 tablespoon dried leaf thyme
1 tablespoon dried leaf oregano
1 teaspoon black pepper
1 teaspoon white pepper
½ teaspoon cayenne pepper

Preparation

1. Measure all of the spices together into an airtight jar. Store away from sunlight and heat until ready to use.

Cajun
Walleye Salad

SIMPLE WALLEYE SALAD SANDWICHES

Yield: 4–6 servings

Simple Walleye Salad Sandwiches

Tired of buying cans of tuna fish when you've got a freezer full of better-tasting fish? Here's a simple way to make a delicious tuna salad substitute—if you want to call something that tastes better than the original a substitute.

Ingredients

1 pound ($\frac{1}{2}$ kg) walleye fillets
1 cup (250 ml) mayonnaise
$\frac{1}{2}$ teaspoon garlic powder
1 tablespoon green jalapeño Tabasco sauce
2 medium cucumbers, peeled and diced
1 cup (250 ml) finely chopped onion
$\frac{3}{4}$ cup (185 ml) finely chopped red bell
    pepper
4–6 deli rolls
3 tomatoes
Lettuce
Slices of sweet Vidalia onions, to taste

Preparation

1. Lay the walleye fillets in a single layer on paper towels or on a plate in the microwave, and cook until they are still moist but fall apart when you try to pick them up; about $1\frac{1}{2}$–2 minutes in a 500-watt unit; 1 minute in a 700-watt microwave. Or you can bake them in a 350°F (175°C) oven for 10 minutes. Chill 1–3 hours.

2. In a medium bowl, combine the mayonnaise, garlic powder, and green sauce, and stir well. Add the cucumber, onion, and red pepper, and toss. Finally, break the chilled fillets into small pieces and fold them into the mayonnaise mixture.

3. To serve, pile the walleye salad on one half of a deli roll, and top with tomato, lettuce, and thinly sliced onions.

WALLEYE CRÊPES
IN PROVOLONE CHEESE SAUCE

Yield: 4 servings

I'll never understand why crêpe gets to be spelled in French while pancake is English. But, they're the same thing: milk, flour, eggs, and a little butter or margarine whipped up in a blender and thrown in a frying pan. The thing is, I don't think I'd ever wrap a pancake around a walleye, but a fillet crêpe? That's out of this world.

Ingredients
2 cups (500 ml) milk
4 eggs
$\frac{2}{3}$ cup (160 ml) sifted flour
4 tablespoons butter or margarine, melted
3 cups (750 ml) diced walleye scraps
2 tablespoons Madeira wine
$\frac{1}{8}$ teaspoon cayenne pepper
$\frac{1}{4}$ teaspoon curry powder
1 tablespoon corn starch
1 cup (250 ml) nonfat yogurt
$\frac{1}{2}$ cup (125 ml) grated provolone cheese

Cooking
1. To make the crêpes, combine the milk, eggs, flour, and 2 tablespoons of the melted butter in a blender or food processor. Purée until smooth, about 10 seconds. In a crêpe pan, low-sided frying pan, or round cast-iron griddle, melt a thin film of butter over medium heat, and pour enough batter onto the pan to make a thin cake. When first adding the batter, tip the pan to distribute it thinly. Cook about 1 minute to brown the first side, then when the crêpe begins to bubble up in the middle, carefully flip it with a spatula, and brown the second side. Continue to make crêpes until all the batter is gone, stacking them on a warm platter.

2. To make the filling, in a large skillet on medium heat, sauté the walleye scraps in 2 tablespoons of butter until the fish is opaque. Add the Madeira and cook until all the liquid is absorbed. Add the cayenne pepper and curry powder, and stir until the fish is coated with the spices. Mix together the corn starch and yogurt and add to the skillet.Continue cooking, stirring continuously, until the sauce is hot. Remove from the heat and stir in the provolone cheese.

3. To assemble, divide the filling equally among the crêpes, laying the filling across the middle of each. Fold each edge over the filling, and serve immediately.

GRILLED WALLEYE WITH HORSERADISH SAUCE

Yield: 6 servings

Walleye (Photo © Doug Stamm)

Serve this dish hot, right off the grill, or chill the extra steaks and bring them along in the cooler on your next fishing excursion. This is one dish that will motivate the anglers to keep their eyes on the line.

Ingredients

$\frac{1}{2}$ cup (125 ml) sour cream
2 tablespoons horseradish
1 teaspoon fresh lemon juice
2 pounds (1 kg) walleye fillet or steaks,
    1 inch (2$\frac{1}{2}$ cm) thick
$\frac{1}{4}$ teaspoon salt
$\frac{1}{4}$ teaspoon pepper

Cooking

1. Soak a handful of apple, hickory, or mesquite wood chips in water, and start about three dozen charcoal briquettes in the barbecue. (Propane units are in retirement for this meal.) Combine the sour cream and horseradish in a small bowl, add the lemon juice, and chill.
2. Pat the fillets dry with paper towels and season with salt and pepper. When the charcoals have white ash over the top, drain the water from the chips, and strew the chips over the coals. Remove the grate and brush lightly with oil. Start the fish immediately. Close the barbecue for maximum smoky flavor.
3. Cook the walleye about 5 minutes to a side, turning once. Serve at once with the horseradish sauce.

Barbecued Walleye Steaks with Tabbouli Salad

Yield: 4–6 servings

If you're watching your fat intake, you can substitute olive oil for the butter in the sauce, but don't leave the sauce out entirely. The combination of sauce and tabbouli salad makes this a dish from the sunny Mediterranean. And, you don't have to heat up the kitchen.

Ingredients
⅓ cup (80 ml) butter or margarine, melted
2 tablespoons fresh lemon juice
1 clove garlic
1 teaspoon dried leaf oregano
1 teaspoon dried leaf basil
2 teaspoons chopped fresh parsley
¼ teaspoon salt
¼ teaspoon pepper
6 walleye steaks, 1 inch (2½ cm) thick

Cooking
1. Combine the butter with lemon juice and stir well. Add the garlic and seasonings, stir, and set aside at room temperature to let the flavors develop.

2. Preheat the propane barbecue or start three dozen charcoal briquettes. When the propane unit has been preheated and turned down to medium high, or the coals are white hot, remove the grill and lightly spray or brush it with oil. This will keep the steaks from sticking.

3. Cook the steaks about 5 minutes to a side, basting with the sauce when you start cooking and again when you turn the steaks. The steaks are done when you insert a fork, turn gently, and the flesh is moist, opaque, and flakes easily. Serve the steaks with more parsley sauce and the following tabbouli salad.

Tabbouli

Yield: 4–6 servings

Ingredients
1 cup (250 ml) dry bulgur
1½ cups (375 ml) boiling water
1 teaspoon salt
¼ cup (60 ml) fresh lemon juice (about 1 lemon)
3 cloves garlic, minced
5 green onions, chopped
1 medium cucumber, peeled and chopped
2 ripe tomatoes, chopped
1 cup (250 ml) minced fresh parsley
2 tablespoons olive oil
½ teaspoon pepper

Preparation
1. Combine the bulgur, boiling water, and salt in a bowl. Cover and set aside about 20 minutes until the bulgur is chewable. Add the rest of the ingredients and chill 2–3 hours before serving.

Note: Bulgur is cracked wheat, a nutty flavored, partially cooked wheat kernel. I love summer salads, and bulgur makes this one easy to fix.

FENNEL BROILED WHOLE WALLEYE

Yield: 4–6 servings

Fennel is an aromatic plant that looks like celery but has a delicate licorice flavor. Trapped in a delicious walleye, it not only adds flavor but moisture to the cooking. Leaving the head on the fish also adds moisture—or prevents it from escaping.

Ingredients

1 whole walleye, 4 pounds (2 kg), with
   head on
2 tablespoons olive oil
2 tablespoons anisette (a licorice-flavored
   liqueur)
½ teaspoon salt
½ teaspoon pepper
5 stalks fresh fennel (green, white, and
   leaves), coarsely chopped

Cooking

1. Preheat the broiler. Rinse the walleye and dry with paper towels. Rub inside and out with the olive oil, then brush the inside with anisette. Season the inside with salt and pepper, then stuff with the fennel. Lay the fish in a shallow, lightly oiled baking pan, and measure the thickness of the belly with a ruler. Insert a meat thermometer, if you're hesitant.

2. Place the fish under the broiler, about 6 inches (15 cm) from the heat. Cook about 10 minutes per 1 inch (2½ cm) of thickness, and baste with pan drippings several times during cooking. Turn over once about halfway through. The thermometer will register 135°F (57°C) internal temperature when done. If not using a thermometer, test for doneness by inserting a fork into the thick flesh of the back and gently twist; fish is done when meat flakes easily, is opaque, and still moist. Serve with risotto and a fresh garden salad.

Note: Fresh fennel is sometimes labeled anise at the grocery store.

Lake fishing (Photo © Doug Stamm)

FABULOUS WALLEYE

Yield: 6–8 servings

This is an adaptation of an old Norwegian recipe, except the natives use all sour cream. I don't like to live that dangerously, so I've added just enough sour cream to taste good, then padded the sauce with nonfat yogurt with a bit of corn starch to keep it stable while baking. Old Norwegians could tell the difference, but if you've never had Fabulous Walleye, you'll never know it's *not* the bad stuff.

Ingredients
2 pounds (1 kg) walleye fillets
3 lemons
$\frac{1}{4}$ cup (60 ml) sour cream
$\frac{1}{2}$ cup (125 ml) nonfat yogurt
1 tablespoon corn starch
1 teaspoon dried tarragon
1 teaspoon salt
$\frac{1}{2}$ teaspoon pepper
3 green onions, chopped

Cooking
1. Preheat the oven to 350°F (175°C). Lay the fillets out in a non-corrosive bowl and squeeze the juice of 2 lemons over the top. (Save the third to slice up for garnish.) Set the fish aside for 10–20 minutes. In a separate bowl, combine the sour cream, yogurt, corn starch, and tarragon, and mix well.
2. Drain the excess liquid off the fish. Place the fish in a shallow baking dish, season with salt and pepper, and pour the sauce over the top. Bake 10–12 minutes. Serve with boiled potatoes and garnish with green onions and sliced lemon.

Fabulous Walleye

WALLEYE FRITTATA

Yield: 4–6 servings

This frittata is rich with eggs and full of strong flavors. Perfect for a late breakfast or early lunch on a lazy day.

Walleye Frittata

Ingredients

1 large red bell pepper, chopped
1 large green bell pepper, chopped
1 medium onion, finely chopped
2 cloves garlic, minced
1 jalapeño pepper, seeded and diced
4 sun-dried tomato halves, broken up
2 tablespoons oil
1 teaspoon dried sweet basil
$\frac{1}{2}$ teaspoon salt
1 teaspoon balsamic vinegar
$\frac{1}{2}$ teaspoon black pepper
4 ounces (100 g) thin spaghetti, cooked
$\frac{3}{4}$ pound (300 g) walleye fillet, cut into
   chunks
4 eggs, beaten
4 ounces (100 g) provolone cheese, shredded
$\frac{1}{2}$ cup (125 ml) grated Parmesan cheese

Cooking

1. Preheat the oven to 350°F (175°C). In a 3- to 5-quart ($2\frac{3}{4}$- to $4\frac{3}{4}$-liter) Dutch oven, sauté the peppers, onion, garlic, jalapeño pepper, and tomato in the oil. Add the basil and salt, and cook, stirring often until the onions and peppers are wilted, about 5–8 minutes. Add the vinegar, half of the black pepper, and spaghetti. Toss lightly, and cook another minute.

2. Add the walleye chunks. Combine the eggs and provolone cheese, and pour that over the vegetables and fish, using the back of a spoon to spread the egg mixture evenly over the top. By now the egg mixture should be starting to set. Remove from the heat. Top with the Parmesan cheese and bake in the oven for 8 minutes or until a toothpick inserted in the center comes out dry.

3. Let stand 10 minutes before serving. Then cut into wedges and serve hot or cool.

WALLEYE PARMESAN

Yield: 4 servings

Since I love veal Parmesan, it was natural for me to try to make walleye taste that good. I'll tell you the truth: It not only tastes good, Walleye Parmesan takes a tenth the time to make. What more could you want?

Ingredients

4 slices white bread
1 teaspoon dried sweet basil
$\frac{1}{2}$ teaspoon dried rosemary
$\frac{1}{4}$ teaspoon ground sage
$\frac{1}{4}$ teaspoon garlic powder
1 teaspoon onion powder
1 egg
1 tablespoon cold water
1 pound ($\frac{1}{2}$ kg) walleye fillets, 1 inch
   ($2\frac{1}{2}$ cm) thick
2 tablespoons olive oil
$\frac{1}{2}$ cup (125 ml) grated Parmesan cheese

Cooking

1. Dry 4 slices of bread in a warm oven for about 1–2 hours. Combine the dried bread, basil, rosemary, sage, and garlic and onion powders in a food processor or blender, and mix thoroughly. Place in a shallow bowl. With a fork, beat together the egg and water in a second bowl. Cut the fillets into four equal pieces, dip each piece in the egg, then coat gently in the bread crumbs.

2. In an 8-inch (20-cm) heavy-bottomed skillet, heat the oil to medium, then place the breaded fish in the pan, one piece at a time. Cook until golden brown and flaky, about 2 minutes to a side. Sprinkle the Parmesan cheese over the top and serve with spaghetti.

Walleye Parmesan

ROAST WALLEYE FILLETS WITH ROASTED POTATOES

Yield: 4 servings

To make this dish work best, cut the fillets so they are the same thickness top to bottom, side to side. Save the leftovers for the Lemon Walleye Stir Fry (page 46). For roasting, it's important for all the fish to cook evenly.

Ingredients

4 medium potatoes, diced

2 tablespoons olive oil

3 cloves garlic, minced

1 tablespoon dried rosemary, crushed

1 pound ($\frac{1}{2}$ kg) walleye fillets, 1 inch ($2\frac{1}{2}$ cm) thick

1 teaspoon salt

1 teaspoon ground pink pepper

2 tablespoons cornmeal

Cooking

1. Preheat the oven to 375°F (190°C). Precook the diced potatoes in boiling water or in the microwave until fork tender.

2. In a shallow baking pan or cast-iron skillet, combine the oil, garlic, and rosemary. Mix well. Lay the fillets in the pan and coat them with the spice-oil mixture on both sides. Pour the potatoes around the fillets, and roll them around in the spices too. Season with salt and pepper.

3. Bake uncovered for 5 minutes. Remove the pan from the oven, sprinkle with the cornmeal, and bake another 15 minutes, until the fish is opaque all the way through, is moist and flakes easily. Serve immediately with salad.

Ice fishing (Photo © Stephen G. Maka— Photo/Nats)

BAKED WALLEYE FILLETS IN TANGERINE SAUCE

Yield: 4 servings

Here's a simple, light, baked dish, with little fat and lots of flavor.

Ingredients

1 pound (½ kg) walleye fillets
½ teaspoon salt
¼ teaspoon black pepper
2 tablespoons fresh lemon juice (about ½ lemon)
½ teaspoon ground coriander
1 medium sweet Vidalia onion, thinly sliced
2 tablespoons chopped fresh cilantro leaves
¾ cup (185 ml) freshly squeezed tangerine juice
¼ cup (60 ml) extra-dry vermouth or dry white wine

Cooking

1. Preheat the oven to 400°F (205°C). In a lightly buttered baking dish, just large enough to hold the fillets, lay the fish out in a single layer. Season with salt and pepper, then drizzle the lemon juice over the top. Sprinkle with coriander, then cover with the onion slices and cilantro leaves. Combine the juice and vermouth, and pour over the top.
2. Bake 20 minutes, uncovered, until the fish is moist but flakes easily. Serve with pasta salad.

Note: Orange juice is an acceptable substitute for tangerine juice, but for a wildly intense substitute use frozen concentrated tangerine or orange juice.

Baked Walleye Fillets in Tangerine Sauce

LEMON WALLEYE STIR FRY

Yield: 4 servings

When you're done cutting 1-inch steaks from your fillets, save the thin, delicate ends for a stir fry. This one is sweet and sour, with a real lemon tang.

*Lemon Walleye
Stir Fry*

Ingredients

1 lemon
2 tablespoons sugar
2 teaspoons corn starch
¼ cup (60 ml) sake (Japanese rice wine)
¼ cup (60 ml) soy sauce
4 ounces (100 g) mushrooms, sliced, about
    1½ cups (375 ml)
1 yellow bell pepper, thinly sliced
1 tablespoon oil
8 green onions, cut into 2-inch (5-cm) lengths
¼ teaspoon black pepper
1½ pounds (¾ kg) walleye bits
4 cups cooked rice

Cooking

1. Grate, zest, or peel (with a potato peeler) the yellow rind from half of the lemon, then juice the lemon. In a small bowl, combine ¼ cup (60 ml) of the lemon juice, and all the sugar, corn starch, sake, soy sauce, and grated lemon peel. Stir well and set aside.

2. In a large skillet over medium-high heat, or in a wok on high, sauté the mushrooms and bell pepper in oil for 1 minute. Add the green onions, black pepper, and diced walleye bits, and cook, stirring constantly, for another minute or two. Add the sake sauce and stir, coating all the ingredients. Cook another 1–2 minutes until the sauce has thickened. Serve over rice.

Walleye fishing (Photo © Doug Stamm)

Steamed Walleye Fishcakes

Yield: 4–6 servings

Lightly browned, then steamed in a rich brown sauce, these fishcakes are light and airy, but loaded with flavor. This is a good way to use those walleyes too small to fillet—or dedicate a whole walleye to the blender. These fishcakes need no excuse.

Steamed Walleye Fishcakes

Ingredients
½ pound (200 g) walleye, cut into chunks
1 medium onion
½ cup (125 ml) milk
2 eggs, separated
1 teaspoon salt
½ teaspoon pepper
⅓ cup (80 ml) instant potato buds
1⅓ cup (320 ml) flour
½ teaspoon curry powder
2 tablespoons oil
1 tablespoon oyster-flavored sauce
1 cup (250 ml) water
6 cups (1½ liters) cooked rice

Cooking
1. Combine the walleye and onion in a food processor or blender and purée. Transfer to a bowl and add the milk, the yolks of both eggs, salt, pepper, and potato buds. Whip the whites of both eggs to stiff peaks, then whip the onion and fish mixture 3 minutes. Fold the egg whites gently into the fish mixture.

2. In a shallow dish, combine the flour and curry powder, then drop a spoonful of the fish mixture into the flour—it will be very loose. Gently pat the mixture with the seasoned flour. When you have a few of these made, heat a frying pan on medium to medium-high heat, add the oil, and lightly brown the outside of the cakes a few a time. You can either transfer them to a warm platter, or pile them up on one side of the pan until you've done all the cakes.

3. Return all the cakes to the pan over medium heat, and distribute them evenly. Combine the oyster-flavored sauce (available in Asian food stores and some fish markets) and water, stir well, and add to the pan. Bring to a slow simmer, cover and cook 15 minutes. To serve, pour the sauce over the fish cakes and rice.

JAMAICAN WALLEYE FRITTERS

Yield: 4–6 servings

Here's something different to serve with those fried eggs next time you go on a camping trip. Make up the fritter batter ahead of time, or make it lakeside, with fresh-caught fish. It's a lot like pancakes but richer tasting.

Ingredients

¼ pound (100 g) walleye fillet, shredded or diced
2 tablespoons lime juice
1 medium onion, chopped
3 green onions, chopped
1 clove garlic, minced
1 tomato, diced
1 jalapeño pepper, cored, seeded, and diced
3 tablespoons oil
1 cup (250 ml) flour
1 teaspoon baking soda
1 teaspoon sweet paprika
1 cup (250 ml) ginger ale, very cold

Cooking

1. Lay the shredded walleye in a shallow bowl and pour the lime juice over the top. Set aside, while you prepare the batter.

2. Sauté the onions, garlic, tomato, and jalapeño pepper in 1 tablespoon of the oil until the onions are soft. Set aside. In a large bowl, sift the flour, baking soda, and paprika together, and add the ginger ale. Stir until well blended, then add the sautéed vegetables. Drain the lime juice off the fish, discard the juice, and add the fish to the batter. Stir well.

3. Start with 1 tablespoon of oil in a skillet over medium-high heat. For each fritter, pour about ¼ cup (60 ml) of batter into the pan, and cook until golden brown, about 2–3 minutes to a side. Add more oil as needed. Serve with a couple of fried eggs, coffee, and fresh oranges.

Jamaican Walleye Fritters

TANGY HAWAIIAN FINGERS

Yield: 4–6 servings

There are two ways you can serve Hawaiian Fingers: slap them on a plate with cole slaw and potato salad, or better yet, find some really good hard-crusted rolls and make yourself a fish sandwich you'll never forget. It's up to you.

Tangy Hawaiian Fingers

Ingredients

1 ¼ cups (310 ml) canned, crushed pineapple, with juice
3 ½ tablespoons sweet hot mustard
½ teaspoon Worcestershire sauce
1 egg
⅔ cup (160 ml) milk
1 cup (250 ml) flour
1 teaspoon sugar
½ teaspoon onion powder
½ teaspoon garlic powder
½ teaspoon pepper
¼ teaspoon dried basil leaves
¼ teaspoon dried thyme leaves
1 pound (½ kg) walleye, cut in 1- by 4-inch (2½- by 10-cm) fingers

Preparation

1. Combine the crushed pineapple, mustard, and Worcestershire sauce in a blender. Purée and set aside.

2. Combine the rest of the ingredients (except the walleye fingers) in a large bowl, mix well, and let sit for 1 hour at room temperature.

Cooking

1. After the batter has set for 1 hour, preheat a deep fat fryer to 370°F (185°C) for 10 minutes. When the fryer is ready, dip each walleye finger into the batter, and fry about 3 minutes until the batter is golden brown and the fish flaky inside. Drain on paper towels and serve with the pineapple-mustard sauce.

WALLEYE BOUILLABAISSE

Yield: 4–6 servings

Here's a light soup with lots of flavor. Slightly French, and definitely delicious, bouillabaisse can be served for lunch; as an appetizer for a holiday dinner; or add a good loaf of garlic bread, and it can be dinner all by itself.

Ingredients

2 cloves garlic, minced

⅔ cup (160 ml) chopped celery

1 medium onion, chopped

1 sweet green pepper, chopped

2 tablespoons oil

1 can whole tomatoes, 14.5 ounces (411 g)

½ teaspoon salt

1 teaspoon sweet paprika

½ cup (125 ml) sherry

3 cups (750 ml) water

1 teaspoon dried leaf oregano

½ teaspoon black pepper

1½ pounds (¾ kg) walleye chunks

Cooking

1. In a heavy-bottomed soup pot, sauté the garlic, celery, onion, and green pepper in the oil until golden brown. Add the tomatoes, salt, paprika, and sherry. Simmer 15 minutes uncovered, then add the water, oregano, and black pepper. Cover and simmer 1 hour.

2. About 5 minutes before serving, add the walleye chunks and stir them into the soup. Serve with garlic bread.

Walleye Bouillabaisse

Chilled White Bass with Shrimp Sauce

Yield: 4 servings

This is perfect for those blah Saturday nights when nothing sounds good to eat—or cook. The shrimp add a bit of sweetness, and the horseradish lights up your get-up-and-go.

Bass fishing at sunset (Photo © Doug Stamm)

Ingredients

½ cup (125 ml) fresh lemon juice (about 2 lemons)

½ cup (125 ml) extra-dry vermouth or sake

1 cup (250 ml) water

¼ cup (60 ml) minced onion

¼ cup (60 ml) minced celery

¼ cup (60 ml) coarsely grated carrot

6 whole peppercorns

¾ teaspoon salt

1 pound (½ kg) white bass fillets, ¾ inch (2 cm) thick

¼ cup (60 ml) nonfat yogurt

¼ cup (60 ml) sour cream

2 teaspoons prepared, cream-style horse-radish

1 teaspoon lime juice

1 green onion, chopped

¼ teaspoon black pepper

1 can medium shrimp, 4½ ounces (120 g), well drained

Cooking

1. Combine the lemon juice, vermouth, water, onion, celery, carrot, peppercorns, and ½ teaspoon only of the salt in a large skillet and bring to a boil. Turn down to a simmer and cook for 20 minutes, covered.

2. Remove the lid, and place the fillets in the braising liquid. Continue simmering until the fish just flakes, about 5 minutes. Turn off the heat and let the fish cool to room temperature in the pan. Then remove the fillets from the cooking liquid and chill. (If you are keeping stock for soups, chowders and other dishes, strain and save this cooking liquid, as well as the shrimp drainings for later use.)

3. In a medium bowl, combine the yogurt, sour cream, horseradish, lime juice, green onion, ¼ teaspoon of salt, and pepper. Stir well, and add the shrimp. Cover and chill 1–2 hours.

4. When all is well chilled, spread the shrimp sauce over the fillets, and serve with fresh garden salad and hard rolls.

BRAISED WHITE BASS FILLETS

Yield: 4 servings

Braising is a low-fat but delicious way to cook fish. Simply sauté a few vegetables, add a little liquid, then bury the fillets in the sauce. Five minutes later, dinner is ready.

Ingredients

1 medium onion
2 cloves garlic
$\frac{1}{2}$ sweet green bell pepper
1 carrot
1 tablespoon butter or margarine
$\frac{1}{2}$ cup (125 ml) fish broth or chicken bouillon
$\frac{1}{2}$ teaspoon dried leaf basil
$\frac{1}{2}$ teaspoon dried leaf marjoram
$\frac{1}{4}$ teaspoon pepper
$\frac{1}{4}$ teaspoon salt
1 teaspoon sugar
1 tablespoon red wine vinegar
1 can diced tomatoes, $14\frac{1}{2}$ ounces (411 g)
1 pound ($\frac{1}{2}$ kg) white bass fillets
4 baked potatoes

Cooking

1. Combine the onion, garlic, bell pepper, and carrot in a food processor and process 3–5 seconds until fine but not puréed.
2. In a medium skillet, sauté the vegetable mixture in the butter until the vegetables are tender. Add the broth, basil, marjoram, pepper, and salt, and simmer until all the excess liquid has been absorbed. Add the sugar, red wine vinegar, tomatoes and their liquid, and bring to a slow simmer.
3. When the braising mixture comes to a simmer, bury the fillets in the simmering vegetables. Cover and simmer for 5 minutes. To serve, break open a baked potato in the bottom of a bowl, lay the fish over the potato, and spoon the sauce over all.

Largemouth bass (Photo © Doug Stamm)

Pᴀsᴛᴀ Pᴇʀᴄʜ *PRIMAVERA*

Yield: 4 servings

A creamy, delicately spiced, warm pasta salad for nights when you want something different without slaving over a hot stove.

Pasta Perch
Primavera

Ingredients

1 clove garlic, minced

1 ½ tablespoons oil

2 shallots, minced

¼ cup (60 ml) extra-dry vermouth

1 ½ tablespoons rice wine vinegar

1 pound (½ kg) perch fillet, diced

4 ounces (100 g) mushrooms, sliced, about
   1 ½ cups (375 ml)

1 green bell pepper, sliced thin

1 cup (250 ml) frozen peas, thawed

½ cup (125 ml) heavy cream

4 ounces (100 g) thin spaghetti, cooked

1 plum tomato, diced

1 teaspoon dried sweet basil

1 teaspoon dried dill weed

1 teaspoon dried leaf tarragon

½ teaspoon salt

½ teaspoon black pepper

½ cup (125 ml) grated Parmesan cheese

Cooking

1. Heat oil to medium-hot in a medium skillet, and sauté the garlic and shallots until soft. Raise the heat to high, and add the vermouth and vinegar. Bring to a simmer. Add the perch, mushrooms, and bell pepper. Cook, stirring often, until the perch is opaque, about 3–4 minutes. Stir in the peas and cream, and simmer until the cream thickens, about 3 minutes.

2. Remove from the heat, and add the spaghetti, tomato, herbs, salt, pepper, and Parmesan cheese. Toss well and serve with hard-crusted bread.

Mexican Perch Tempura with Homemade French Fries

Yield: 6–8 servings

No, these aren't an exotic perch from Mexico. And the tempura is still Japanese—although by way of Mexico. An international dish that's as American as French fries.

Ingredients

2 egg yolks
1 whole egg
1 cup (250 ml) cold water
¾ cup (185 ml) salsa
1 teaspoon ground cumin
¼ teaspoon pepper
1 cup (250 ml) flour
2 pounds (1 kg) perch
8 large white potatoes, scrubbed or peeled

Cooking

1. In a blender or food processor, combine the egg yolks, egg, water, and salsa, and purée 5 seconds. Pour into a large mixing bowl, and add the cumin and pepper. With a fork, gradually stir in the flour, but do not overstir—there should even be a little flour floating on top—in order to make a light batter.

2. Cut the perch into bite-sized chunks no larger than ½ inch (1 cm) thick and 1½ inches (3½ cm) long and wide. Pat dry with a paper towel. Cut the potatoes into ¼-inch (½-cm) strips for fries and pat them dry, too.

3. Using a deep-fat fryer or electric skillet with enough cooking oil to cover the fish completely, heat the oil to 375°F (190°C). (Most one-temperature fryers automatically cook at that temperature.) Dip the fish in the tempura batter, then lower them gently into the fryer; fry 5 minutes, or until golden brown. Remove cooked pieces to a paper towel to drain briefly.

4. When all the fish is done (or alternately cook fish and potatoes in serving-sized batches if someone can't wait), add the potatoes in four batches, and cook each 5 minutes, or until golden brown and floating on top. Serve the fries with ketchup; the Mexican Tempura needs no sauce.

Mexican Perch Tempura with Homemade French Fries

BASS CROQUETTES

Yield: 4 servings

Here's a great appetizer for your next party: a bite-sized, flavor-packed, hot hors d'oeuvre. No need for dipping sauce, either; they stand up quite nicely on their own. Don't be intimidated by the long list of ingredients: You sauté some vegetables, make a simple white sauce, then drop a few fish balls in a deep-fat fryer. It's really quite straightforward.

Bass Croquettes

Ingredients

3 cloves garlic, minced
$\frac{1}{2}$ cup (125 ml) finely chopped onion
$\frac{1}{4}$ cup (60 ml) finely chopped celery
$\frac{1}{4}$ cup (60 ml) finely chopped green pepper
$\frac{1}{2}$ cup (125 ml) diced tomato
1 tablespoon oil
$\frac{1}{2}$ teaspoon dried leaf marjoram
1 teaspoon dried dill weed
$\frac{1}{2}$ teaspoon salt

$\frac{1}{4}$ teaspoon pepper
2 slices bread, white or wheat
$\frac{1}{2}$ cup (125 ml) milk
2 tablespoons butter or margarine
2 tablespoons flour
1 cup (250 ml) milk
2 tablespoons Madeira
2 cups (500 ml) fish bits
1 cup (250 ml) cornmeal

Ice fishing (Photo © Bill Marchel)

Cooking

1. In a large skillet, sauté the garlic, onion, celery, green pepper, and tomato in oil until lightly browned. Add the marjoram, dill, salt, and pepper, and stir to coat the vegetables. Remove from the heat. In a shallow bowl, combine the bread and milk, and let sit for 10 minutes, until the bread has absorbed the milk. Squeeze the excess milk off the bread, add the bread to the vegetables, and mix well together. The milk-soaked bread acts to bind together the croquettes.

2. To make the white sauce, melt the butter in a small saucepan over medium heat. Add the flour and stir until the mixture is smooth and golden. Slowly add the milk as you stir, then cook over low heat, stirring for 7–10 minutes until the sauce is thick. Pour the sauce into the sautéed vegetables, add the Madeira and fish, and stir gently. Spread the mixture out in a shallow baking dish and chill for 60 minutes.

3. Pour the cornmeal into a shallow bowl and set aside. Once the croquette mixture has chilled, shape it into $1\frac{1}{2}$-inch ($3\frac{1}{2}$-cm) balls. Lower them carefully into a deep-fat fryer with enough cooking oil to cover at 370°F (190°C), and cook a few at a time for about 3 minutes each, or until crisp and brown. Roll in the cornmeal and serve immediately.

SZECHUAN BASS STIR FRY

Yield: 4 servings

Szechuan cooking is, by tradition, hot, but this dish is not firehouse hot. If you want to up the temperature, add more ginger in the sauce and red pepper flakes at the end. For the rest of us, this is a warm, but comfortable, taste of the exotic.

Szechuan Bass Stir Fry

Ingredients

1 tablespoon corn starch
2 teaspoons sugar
$\frac{1}{4}$ cup (60 ml) sake or dry sherry
3 tablespoons soy sauce
$\frac{1}{4}$ cup (60 ml) orange juice
1 teaspoon ground ginger
1 tablespoon oil
3 cloves garlic, minced
1 medium onion, coarsely chopped
4 ounces (100 g) pea pods
4 ounces (100 g) broccoli flowerets, separated
$\frac{1}{2}$ medium red bell pepper, sliced thin
1 pound ($\frac{1}{2}$ kg) bass fillet pieces
Dash of red pepper flakes

Cooking

1. In a small bowl, combine the corn starch, sugar, sake, soy sauce, orange juice, and ginger. Stir well and set aside.

2. In a large skillet or wok, heat the oil on medium high. Quickly stir-fry the garlic and onions until tender. Add the pea pods, broccoli, and sliced pepper. Cover and cook about 5 minutes until the vegetables are tender, but still crisp. Add the fish and ginger sauce, stirring to coat all the ingredients well. Cook until the fish turns opaque. Finish with a dash of red pepper flakes, and serve over rice.

Basso Bass

Yield: 4–6 servings

Madeira wine always reminds me of the beautiful, resonant voice of the bass singer in a quartet. Partly it's the deep, dark color, but mainly it's the taste. When you cook with Madeira, you end up with a complex, resonant, full-bodied flavor that's hard to imitate. Basso Bass will make you feel like a real chef, and since it's fish, you're in and out of the kitchen in 20 minutes.

Ingredients

4 tablespoons butter

⅛ teaspoon curry powder

2 ounces (50 g) or ¾ cup (185 ml) mushrooms, sliced

2 shallots, minced

½ cup (125 ml) finely chopped onions

⅓ cup (80 ml) Madeira

½ pound (250 g) bass fillet, cut into 1-inch (2½-cm) chunks

1 egg yolk

½ cup (125 ml) fish stock (see page 74), or bottled clam juice

Cooking

1. Melt the butter in an 8-inch (20-cm) skillet on low heat. Add the curry powder, and when you can smell the curry aroma, bring the temperature up to medium and sauté the mushrooms, shallots, and onions until tender, about 5 minutes. Add the Madeira and diced bass, stir to coat, and simmer 5 minutes.

2. In a small bowl, lightly beat the egg yolk, add the fish stock, mix, and pour into the skillet. Bring the mixture back to a simmer, and cook 2 more minutes until the juices have thickened. Serve immediately over rice.

Basso Bass

CREOLE CORN AND BASS CASSEROLE

Yield: 4–6 servings

This is one of those old-fashioned, one-dish, stick-to-your-rib meals that seems to be making a comeback in the nether world of urban America. Fortunately, the casserole never really died in the West and Midwest. Just go to any church or community pot luck: rich, heavy casseroles are still king of the hill.

Bass fishing (Photo © Doug Stamm)

Ingredients

1 medium onion, chopped
5 cloves garlic, minced
1 green bell pepper, chopped
1 tablespoon oil
3 cups (750 ml) frozen corn, thawed
½ teaspoon salt
¼ teaspoon black pepper
¼ teaspoon cayenne pepper
½ teaspoon dried oregano leaves
¼ teaspoon dried thyme leaves
1½ pound (¾ kg) fillets, cut into chunks
½ cup (125 ml) cornmeal
1 egg, slightly beaten
2 cups (500 ml) milk

Cooking

1. Preheat the oven to 350°F (175°C). In a large skillet, sauté the onion, garlic, and green pepper in oil until browned. Add the corn and seasonings, and stir well. When the mixture is sizzling again in the pan, stir in the fish chunks and cornmeal. In a small bowl, combine the egg and milk; pour into the pan and stir.
2. Place in a deep 3-quart (2¾-liter) casserole, and bake uncovered for 1 hour.

BAKED BASS FILLETS WITH PARSLEY AND CREAM

Yield: 4 servings

If you are lucky enough to have bass in your favorite fishing spot, take them home and bake them in this rich, stick-to-your-ribs sauce. The best part is that the sauce makes itself.

Ingredients

2 pounds (1 kg) bass fillets
3 tablespoons butter or margarine, softened
1 teaspoon salt
$\frac{1}{2}$ teaspoon pepper
1 can chopped tomatoes, 28 ounces (795 g)
1 tablespoon parsley flakes (1 teaspoon if fresh)
1 teaspoon sugar
1 medium onion, thinly sliced
1 teaspoon sweet Hungarian paprika
$\frac{2}{3}$ cup (160 ml) heavy cream

Cooking

1. Preheat the oven to 400°F (205°C). Pat the fillets dry with paper towels, place them in a single layer in a buttered baking dish, and brush with the remaining butter. Sprinkle with salt and pepper. In a small bowl, combine the tomatoes, parsley, and sugar, and pour over the top of the fillets. Cover with the sliced onion.

2. Bake uncovered for 20 minutes. Then combine the paprika and cream, and pour over the top. Bake another 10 minutes. Serve with mashed potatoes, made with half white potatoes and half rutabagas—trust me; you won't need to smother them with butter.

Smallmouth bass (Photo © Doug Stamm)

BAKED BASS AND GUACAMOLE HEROES

Yield: 4 servings

Roll the fillets in spicy bread crumbs and bake, not fry, 12 minutes; then unbutton one avocado, and add a little nonfat yogurt, buttermilk, or for the really daring, mayonnaise. Once you taste one of these heroes you'll understand why everyone tried to grow avocado trees in the fifties.

Baked Bass and Guacamole Heroes

Ingredients

2 ripe avocados

3 tablespoons nonfat yogurt, buttermilk, or mayonnaise

2 teaspoons fresh lemon juice

10 drops red pepper Tabasco sauce

$\frac{1}{2}$ cup (125 ml) bread crumbs

$\frac{1}{2}$ teaspoon dried sweet basil leaves

$\frac{1}{8}$ teaspoon garlic powder

$\frac{1}{4}$ teaspoon ground cumin

$\frac{1}{2}$ teaspoon chili powder

3 tablespoons nonfat yogurt or buttermilk

4 catfish fillets, 4–6 ounce (100–200 g) each, $\frac{1}{2}$ inch (1 cm) thick

4 deli rolls, long enough to fit the fillet

2 ripe tomatoes, sliced (optional)

Cooking

1. In a shallow bowl or plate, mash the avocado flesh with a fork. Stir in 3 tablespoons of the yogurt, all the lemon juice, and the Tabasco sauce. Cover tightly, and chill 1–3 hours.

2. Preheat the oven to 450°F (235°C). Combine the bread crumbs, basil, garlic, cumin, and chili powder in a shallow bowl. Measure the last 3 tablespoons of yogurt into a second bowl. (Do not substitute mayonnaise here—the coating needs to be thin.) Trim the fillets. Dip them into the yogurt, then the bread crumbs, pressing the bread-crumb coating into the flesh with the back of a spoon. Place the fillets on a foil-lined baking sheet.

3. Place the baking sheet in the center of the oven, and bake 12 minutes. If you want to heat the deli rolls, split them, and place them in the oven for the last 4–5 minutes of cooking.

4. To serve, place the fillets on the bottom half of the roll, add a few slices of tomato, and spoon the guacamole on the top. Enjoy.

Fried Catfish and Hush Puppies

Yield: 4 servings

A traditional, fried catfish meal. They're not perfectly round like the hush puppies at the Tastee Freeze stand at Gulf Shores, Mobile, Alabama, but they're good.

Hush Puppies Ingredients

1 ½ cups (375 ml) cornmeal
½ cup (125 ml) white flour
1 tablespoon baking powder
¼ teaspoon dried leaf oregano
¼ teaspoon dried thyme leaves
⅛ teaspoon cayenne pepper
⅛ teaspoon black pepper
¼ teaspoon salt
¼ cup (60 ml) diced onion
1 cup (125 ml) milk
1 egg

Catfish Ingredients

1 egg
½ cup (125 ml) milk
1 tablespoon country Dijon mustard
1 cup (250 ml) cornmeal
1 cup (250 ml) white flour
4 teaspoons Cajun Shake (see recipe on page 35)
1 pound (½ kg) catfish fillets

Cooking the Hush Puppies

In a medium bowl, combine all the dry ingredients and onion. In a separate bowl, combine the milk and egg, beat lightly together, and stir in the dry ingredients. Fill a skillet or deep-fat fryer with 2 inches (5 cm) of cooking oil and preheat to 375°F (190°C). Drop the batter from a tablespoon into the hot fat and cook for 3 minutes or until golden brown. Drain the hush puppies on paper towels and keep them warm while you cook the fish.

Cooking the Catfish

1. In a shallow bowl, combine the egg, milk, and mustard, and beat lightly until mixed. In a second shallow bowl, combine the cornmeal, flour, and Cajun Shake.
2. Cut the catfish into 1- by 2-inch (2½- by 5-cm) pieces, roll in the cornmeal mixture, then in the milk, then again in the cornmeal. The second time, press the cornmeal into the catfish pieces for a good coating. Fry the catfish in the 375°F (190°C) fat in small batches for 3 minutes or until golden brown. Serve the hush puppies and catfish with a green salad.

CATFISH *CHILAQUILES*

Yield: 4 servings

Fishing at dusk (Photo © Doug Stamm)

Chilaquiles is a rich, south-of-the-border baked dish that will ease your post-fishing-season withdrawal symptoms. If this doesn't do it, you may need to take drastic steps—like flying to the southern hemisphere—where it's summer—with your favorite fishing partner.

Ingredients

1 large onion, coarsely chopped
2 tablespoons oil
1 pound (½ kg) ripe tomatoes
4 teaspoons (or 2 whole) diced jalapeño peppers
¼ cup (60 ml) chopped fresh cilantro leaves
1⅓ cup (325 ml) tomato sauce
½ cup (125 ml) water
1 teaspoon salt
8 corn tortillas, torn in strips
1 pound (½ kg) Monterey Jack cheese, grated
1½ pound (¾ kg) catfish fillet, chopped
½ cup (125 ml) milk
½ cup (125 ml) sour cream

Cooking

1. In a medium skillet, sauté the onion in the oil until golden brown. Add the tomatoes, jalapeño, cilantro, tomato sauce, water, and salt, and simmer about 10 minutes uncovered.

2. Preheat the oven to 375°F (190°C). In a deep casserole dish, spoon a little sauce on the bottom, then cover with a third of the tortilla strips. Top that with a third of the cheese, fish, and sauce. Make two more layers of the tortillas, cheese, fish, and sauce. In a small bowl, combine the milk and sour cream, and pour it over the top of the stack, letting it seep down into the sides and cracks of the casserole.

3. Cover and bake 20 minutes; then uncover and bake another 10. Let stand about 10 minutes before serving.

CLAY POT CATFISH FILLETS

Yield: 4 servings

So if fish cooks so fast, why cook it in a clay pot? Wouldn't that take longer than 10 minutes per inch? Well, yes. But the clay pot, as always, ensures a perfectly moist fillet. And the sweet hot mustard sauce gives it a real zip.

Fishing at the "magic hour" (Photo © Bill Marchel)

Ingredients
3 tablespoons butter or margarine
3 tablespoons rice-wine vinegar
3 tablespoons dry mustard
2 tablespoons sugar
1 tablespoon corn starch, dissolved in
    1 tablespoon cold water
2 pounds (1 kg) catfish fillets, 1 inch (2 ½ cm) thick

Cooking
1. Melt the butter in a saucepan and add the vinegar, mustard, sugar, and corn starch mixture. Cook over medium-high heat (or in a microwave, 30 seconds at a time) until the mixture comes to a boil, stirring constantly until it thickens. Cool the sauce in the refrigerator 20–30 minutes while you prepare the clay pot.
2. Soak the clay pot in cool water for 15 minutes. Lay the fillets in the bottom of the pot, spreading the mustard sauce on each fillet until it is all used. Cover and place the pot in a cold oven; do not preheat. Then, if you are using an electric oven, turn the heat to 450°F (235°C). If you are using a gas oven, turn the heat on low, then over 5–10 minutes, gradually raise the temperature until you reach 450°F (235°C).
3. Bake 30 minutes or until the fillets are flaky. Serve with rice and fresh green beans.

CURRIED CATFISH

Yield: 4 servings

If you're like me and don't like that sickeningly sweet stuff candy makers call coconut, you may be surprised to learn that fresh coconut—and unsweetened coconut milk—doesn't taste anything like that. You can buy unsweetened coconut milk in the ethnic section of your grocery store, with the Asian foods, and it was made to go with curry. Like the proverbial horse and carriage, coconut milk and curry is a taste that was always meant to go together. They've known this in India, Asia, and Africa for centuries, and now it comes here to catfish.

Curried Catfish

Ingredients
½ cup (125 ml) diced onion
½ red bell pepper, diced
1 teaspoon curry powder
3 tablespoons butter or margarine
1 ½ cups (375 ml) unsweetened coconut milk
1 ½ pounds (¾ kg) catfish chunks
2 cups (500 ml) cooked rice

Cooking
1. In a medium skillet, sauté the onion, red bell pepper, and curry powder in the butter until the onions are soft. Add the coconut milk and simmer 10 minutes until thickened.
2. Add the fish chunks and cooked rice, and simmer another 5 minutes until the fish is opaque and the rice is hot. Serve with fresh sliced tomatoes, cucumbers, and red pepper.

CATFISH GUMBO

Yield: 4–6 servings

For all those people who prefer their food hot and spicy, gumbo is the dish for you. With white pepper, cayenne pepper, and just a touch of Tabasco sauce, this isn't tame. For the rest of us, add the peppers cautiously—but add some, so you get the flavor of a true American classic.

Ingredients

1½ teaspoons sweet paprika
½ teaspoon white pepper
½ teaspoon dried leaf thyme
½ teaspoon dried leaf oregano
1 bay leaf, crumbled
¼ teaspoon cayenne pepper
2 cups (500 ml) finely chopped onions
2 cups (500 ml) finely chopped celery
1 sweet bell pepper, chopped
4 tablespoons margarine (not butter)
2 cloves garlic, minced
1 teaspoon red pepper Tabasco sauce
2 tablespoons file gumbo powder
1¼ cups (300 ml) tomato sauce
1 cup (250 ml) water
1 jar of clam juice, 8 ounces (200 g)
1 can or bottle of beer, 12 ounces (360 ml)
2 cups (500 ml) cooked rice
1½ pounds (675 g) catfish fillets, cut into chunks

Cooking

1. In a small bowl, combine the paprika, white pepper, thyme, oregano, bay leaf, and cayenne pepper, and mix well. Set aside.

2. In a medium skillet over medium heat, sauté the onions, celery, and green peppers in margarine until tender. Increase the heat to high, and add the garlic, Tabasco sauce, file gumbo, and the paprika-spice mix. Cook for 4 minutes on high, stirring constantly, and scraping the sauce up from the bottom of the pan. Reduce the heat to medium, and add the tomato sauce. Cook 3 minutes more, until the sauce sticks to the bottom of the pan, then add the water, clam juice, and beer. Cover and simmer 45 minutes.

3. Add the rice and catfish chunks. Turn the heat off immediately, cover the pot, and let the rice and fish poach for 5–10 minutes.

Catfish Gumbo

RED PEPPER AND CATFISH SOUP

Yield: 4 servings

Red Pepper and Catfish Soup

You can use any white-fleshed fish for this soup; I just happened to have a bunch of catfish fillets in the freezer. With the fish, potatoes, and peppers, it's a complete meal, and one that will warm anybody up on a cold, rainy day.

Ingredients

1 onion, chopped

¼ pound (100 g) mushrooms, sliced, about 1½ cups (375 ml)

2 large red bell peppers, sliced

1 ripe tomato, sliced

1 pound (½ kg) catfish fillets, cut into chunks

2 tablespoons oil

2 cups (500 ml) fish stock (see page 74), or chicken broth

2 medium potatoes, peeled and sliced thin

½ cup (125 ml) whipping cream

¼ teaspoon salt

¼ teaspoon red pepper flakes

Cooking

1. In a medium skillet, sauté the onion, mushrooms, peppers, tomato, and fish chunks in oil until the onions and pepper are tender, about 10 minutes. Add the fish stock and potatoes, and bring to a boil. Reduce the heat and simmer, uncovered, for 15 minutes, until the potato slices break up easily when stirred.

2. Remove the soup from the heat, and let cool for about 15 minutes, or until it is safe to put in the food processor or blender. Purée the soup, and return it to the pot.

3. Bring the soup back to a simmer. Add the cream, salt, and pepper flakes (add more, to taste), and serve immediately, with hard rolls and a grating of Parmesan cheese if desired.

Wading angler at the "magic hour" (Photo © Bill Marchel)

BAKE AND FLAKE MEXICAN PANFISH CASSEROLE

Yield: 2 servings

Mexican casserole is a one-dish meal that you can make for two or for a crowd. Make this recipe in a small casserole or triple it for a 9x13-inch (22x32-cm) baking pan. Either way, it is a different way to enjoy panfish.

Ingredients

½ medium onion, chopped
2 cloves garlic, minced
1 tablespoon oil
¾ teaspoon ground cumin
¼ teaspoon pepper
½ teaspoon chili powder
½ teaspoon dried leaf oregano

⅛ teaspoon red pepper flakes
1 can whole tomatoes, 16 ounces (454 g)
1 teaspoon green jalapeño Tabasco sauce
½ cup (125 ml) frozen corn, thawed
1½ cups (375 ml) cooked rice
8 ounces (200 g) flaked panfish meat
4 ounces (100 g) medium Cheddar cheese, coarsely grated

Bluegill fishing (Photo © Doug Stamm)

Cooking

1. Preheat oven to 350°F (175°C). In a large skillet, sauté the onion and garlic in oil, then add the seasonings and stir to coat the vegetables.
2. In a large bowl, combine the tomatoes with their juice, the Tabasco sauce, and onion mixture. Stir well, then add the corn, rice, flaked fish, and two-thirds of the cheese, and toss gently.
3. Pour into a 1½-quart (1¼-liter) casserole, cover with the remaining cheese, and bake, uncovered, for 30 minutes. Serve with tortilla chips.

Note: To bake and flake the fish, preheat the oven to 350°F (175°C). Place the cleaned panfish on a lightly oiled or foil-lined baking sheet, and place in the center of the oven. Bake just long enough so that you can lift the skin off the fish. Follow the 10 minutes per 1 inch (2½ cm) of thickness rule, and remember that a lot of panfish aren't an inch thick. Remove the fish from the oven, skin, and flake the meat off the bones.

Cajun Fried Panfish with New Potatoes and Peas

Yield: 4 servings

There are certain times of the year when the stars collide, and all things seem possible. Gardeners know that that time is July, when the pea pods are fat. They steal a few immature potatoes from the fall harvest, catch a fish, and have the most delicious and deserved dinner of the harvest year: panfish and new potatoes with peas. If you work it right, you many not have any mature potatoes left for fall harvest, but there will always be more panfish.

New Potato Ingredients

2 pounds (1 kg) new potatoes, scrubbed or peeled
1 pound ($\frac{1}{2}$ kg) freshly shucked peas
3 tablespoons butter or margarine
3 tablespoons flour
$1\frac{1}{3}$ cup (330 ml) milk
$\frac{1}{2}$ teaspoon salt
$\frac{1}{2}$ teaspoon pepper

Fish Ingredients

6–8 bluegills or other panfish, cleaned
1 cup (250 ml) flour
2 teaspoons Cajun Shake (see recipe on page 35)
Peanut oil

Cooking the Potatoes

1. Boil the new potatoes until fork tender. Drain the water into another pot. Cover the potatoes, and set aside to keep warm. In the second pot, pour the peas into the potato water, and simmer 5 minutes until they are bright green. Drain and add the peas to the potatoes.
2. In a medium saucepan over medium heat, melt the butter, then stir in the flour until the mixture is smooth. Increase the heat to medium-high, and when the mixture starts to bubble, slowly add the milk, stirring constantly. Continue stirring until the sauce is thick, then pour it over the potatoes and peas, and toss gently to coat. Season with salt and pepper. Cover and keep warm.

Cooking the Fish

1. Pat the panfish dry with paper towels. Combine the flour and Cajun Shake seasoning, and dredge the fish in this mixture.
2. Fill a large skillet with 1 inch ($2\frac{1}{2}$ cm) of peanut oil. Heat the oil to the smoking point, then turn the heat down slightly, so the oil just stops smoking. Gently slip the fish into the pan, two or three at a time, leaving room in the pan so they won't touch. The coating will get crunchy almost immediately if the oil is hot enough. Turn as soon as the first side is golden brown, and remove when the second side is golden as well. There's no trick to this: Just don't overcook them, or cook them in oil that is too cool as hot oil means that less oil is absorbed into the flesh.
3. Place the fried fish on paper towels until the whole batch is ready, then serve with the new potatoes and a fresh garden salad.

Easy Panfish Pie

Yield: 3–6 servings

You don't have to make this as a pie; simply pour the fish and sauce over rice if you want, but frozen pastry shells are an easy way to fancy-up a dish without spending a lot of time in the kitchen. And don't get put off by first impressions: frozen, those pastry shells look more like hockey pucks than supper; cooked, they're a sweet contrast to the tart flavor of this sauce.

Easy Panfish Pie

Ingredients

6 frozen pastry shells
½ medium onion, chopped
1 tablespoon oil
½ teaspoon dried thyme leaves
1 teaspoon ground coriander
½ teaspoon ground mustard powder
¾ teaspoon sweet paprika

½ teaspoon salt
¼ teaspoon pepper
3 tablespoons flour
1 can or bottle of beer, 12 ounces (360 ml)
1 cup (250 ml) thinly sliced carrots
1 cup (250 ml) peas
1 pound (½ kg) flaked panfish meat

Cooking

1. Bake the pastry shells according to package directions, about 25 minutes.

2. In the meantime, in a medium skillet over medium-high heat, sauté the onion in oil until soft. Add the spices and stir to coat the onions. Sprinkle the flour, 1 tablespoon at a time, over the onions stirring as you add. The mixture will get very dry. Once all the flour is stuck to the onions, slowly add the beer, stirring as you add. Bring to a simmer, and let the sauce thicken as you stir. As the sauce thickens, steam or microwave the carrots and peas until the carrots are fork tender and the peas are bright green, about 1–2 minutes, then add them to the mixture. Add the fish, and continue simmering until the fish flakes are hot again.

3. To serve, pour the fish mixture into the pastry shells, and serve immediately.

Note: To bake and flake the fish, preheat the oven to 375°F (190°C). Place the cleaned panfish on a lightly oiled or foil-lined baking sheet, and place in the center of the oven. Bake just long enough so that you can lift the skin off the fish. Follow the 10 minutes per 1 inch (2 ½ cm) of thickness rule, and remember that a lot of panfish aren't an inch thick. Remove the fish from the oven, skin, and flake the meat off the bones.

Sunfish catch after a day ice fishing (Photo © Bill Marchel)

FISH STOCK

Yield: 1½ quarts (1¼ liters)

Stock is an ongoing masterpiece: whatever fish you have on hand, whatever you can spare to the pot, plus the odd onion, carrot, and spice. If you want to make it with a south-of-the-border taste, add 1 teaspoon each of cumin and chili powder, then a sprinkling of red pepper flakes, or, for special occasions, saffron. For a European flavor, try equal amounts of rosemary, thyme, basil, tarragon, and summer savory. I save the shells from our occasional shrimp dinners to make a richer stock. Stock is whatever you want. But don't add salt to a basic stock: The ingredients will have a certain amount of natural salt, which is then cooked down and concentrated. Add the salt later when you use the stock to make soup or stew. Here's a good basic recipe to get started.

Ingredients
3 pounds (1½ kg) fish heads and bones
1 onion, chopped
1 carrot, chopped
¼ cup fresh lemon juice (about 1 lemon)
   2 quarts (2 liters) water
10 peppercorns, lightly crushed
1 teaspoon yellow mustard seeds
½ cup (125 ml) chopped parsley

Cooking
1. Wash and rinse the fish heads and bones; remove all entrails, gills, and skin. Place the fish, onion, carrot, lemon juice, and water into a soup pot, bring to a boil, and skim any foam from the surface of the water. Reduce to a simmer and add the rest of the ingredients. Cover, and simmer 45 minutes.

2. After 45 minutes, strain the liquid off, and discard the solids and spices. Use the stock immediately, or refrigerate up to 3 days. You can also freeze the stock in ice cube trays, then transfer to resealable plastic bags and freeze for up to 3 months. Use in any recipe calling for fish stock or broth.

Bluegill (Photo © Doug Stamm)

SALMON AND STEELHEAD

There's an old fishing joke about a fly fisherman who dies and wakes up on the other side, standing in a trout stream in Scotland, a grizzled, tweedy guide handing him a rigged fly rod. With his first cast, the angler catches a ten-pound salmon; with his second another ten-pound beauty. Three, six, eight casts later, he's still catching these magnificent lunker salmon, and he turns to his guide and says, "You'd think if heaven was perfect, God would vary the size of these fish." The guide takes his meerschaum pipe out of his mouth for just a second and mumbles, "Nobody said this was heaven."

Being into fly fishing myself, and loving those silly rainbow trout in small mountain streams, I'd never truly understood the joke for many years. Too many fish? A fish on every cast? That couldn't be part of the joke. But then I fished for king salmon on a remote stream in Alaska and realized there is a point at which even catching a fish on every cast isn't exactly fun anymore. When each of those fish weighs more than twenty-five pounds (12 kg), there actually is a limit to how much fun a person can have in one day—if you want to have the use of both arms for the rest of your life. But when it comes to the freezer, that sacrifice may be worth it.

There are five varieties of Pacific salmon found in North America. A sixth, cherry salmon, is found in Asia. Atlantic salmon have been almost entirely reduced to farm fish or catch-and-release fishing. While some may say steelhead don't belong in this chapter, they are more like salmon in size, taste, and cooking methods than they are like their near relative, the rainbow trout, and are migratory as well. If it looks, tastes, and cooks like a salmon, then in this book, it is a salmon.

All Pacific salmon are born in fresh water, run to the sea, and then return to their birth streams to spawn. After this similarity, though, the variations are endless. Fall chinooks go to sea three to four months after birth, while coho, spring chinooks, and sockeye wait a year or more. The length of their stay in the ocean varies as well. Coho spend only two years at sea and never stray very far from the mouth of their birth streams. Sockeyes stay in the Pacific Ocean for seven to eight years and have been sighted halfway to China, and chinooks travel as much as twenty-five hundred miles in their saltwater sojourn. Kokanee, a land-locked sockeye, is considered a Pacific salmon even though it never sets fin in salt water. That may seem confusing, but if you ever bite into a dark red kokanee, you will taste salmon.

The big mystery has always been how a fish that travels as much as twenty-five hundred miles from home and stays away for up to eight years, then unerringly returns to the hundred yards of coast that forms the mouth of its birth river. Scientists know salmon can smell their home waters once they get there, and surmise that the iron in their systems reacts with the earth's magnetic field, like a compass. Unsubstantiated reports claim that migratory salmon invented the global positioning system (GPS) long before mere mortal did, but, of course, no one has proven that.

Unfortunately the GPS is no good for helping Pacific salmon find their way through a maze of dams, over-zealous anglers, pollution, and habitat destruction. They have taken a beating over the last fifty years, especially in the southern end of their range. But the coho salmon may have been fortuitously blessed: It likes a short spawning commute, and is attracted to small streams of little value to hydroelectric development and agricultural irrigation. Other salmon are marathon runners: I have heard of twelve-pounders (6-kg fish) being caught as far upstream as the Continental Divide near the Montana border, which meant a run across the states of Washington and Idaho. In the last century, that wasn't much of a commute, but now it's deadly.

Atlantic salmon are almost a totally catch-and-release proposition; commercial fishing is dead, and the only Atlantic salmon you find in stores have been farm-raised. Alaska is about the only place you can still go to have too much fun salmon fishing. In the seventeenth and eighteenth centuries, we cut down all the best British oaks; when they were gone, the white pines in New England went; in 1925, when the *U.S. Constitution* needed a new set of hundred-foot masts, the Douglas fir of the Pacific Northwest was the only tree left that was tall enough. If salmon are as renewable a resource as trees, Alaska should be careful.

King (Chinook) Salmon

Kings are the largest and most popular eating of all wild salmon. They have the darkest flesh, though not the firmest, and have about 7 to 15 percent fat content. One reason for their popularity is that, despite their long migrations, they do not become as quickly emaciated as other salmon on their spawning runs. Female kings, especially, have been caught healthy and plump five hundred miles up their natal streams. Kings are also the largest salmon, growing up to 100 pounds (50 kg), with the average catch being about 18 pounds (9 kg).

Sockeye (Red) Salmon

Like kings, sockeye have a high fat content and deep-red flesh, but aren't nearly so large. The largest sockeye caught on rod and reel weighed $15\frac{1}{2}$ pounds ($7\frac{3}{4}$ kg), while an average fish runs about 5 to 7 pounds ($2\frac{1}{2}$ to $3\frac{1}{2}$ kg).

Kokanee Salmon

Kokanee are the land-locked version of sockeye, and share their dark flesh and high oil content. Like all salmon, their diet is mostly crustaceans. They are the only salmon to mature in fresh water, and kokanee are extremely popular among sport anglers because they are delicious to eat, plentiful, and easy to catch. They also live a lot closer to home. A record kokanee is 4 pounds (2 kg), while the average catch varies in length from 8 to 24 inches (20 to 60 cm), depending on the quality of feed in their habitat.

Coho Salmon

Coho have medium-red flesh and a lower fat content than do king, sockeye, and kokanee salmon, which makes them less desirable as table fare, but quite good nonetheless. The record coho weighed 33 pounds ($16\frac{1}{2}$ kg), but the average catch is more like 8 to 18 pounds (4 to 9 kg).

Chum

Chum salmon are rarely taken by sport anglers. Their pale-pink flesh and low fat content (less than 4 percent) add up to less flavor. In fact, their nickname, dog salmon, comes from the Inuit habit of feeding chum to their dogs. Like coho, chum can reach more than 30 pounds (15 kg), but average 6 to 12 pounds (3 to 6 kg).

Steelhead

Steelhead are rainbow trout that go to the ocean and then return to their natal streams to spawn. In size and taste they are more like salmon than trout, but like trout (and Atlantic salmon), they can spawn several times. To make things more confusing, biologists now classify rainbows as Pacific salmon and have given them all—Pacific salmon, cutthroat, and rainbow trout—the same generic name, *Oncorhynchus*. Steelhead can and should be cooked like salmon. Size varies according to fisheries, but most fish will weigh 6 to 15 pounds (3 to $5\frac{1}{2}$ kg).

Transporting Fresh Salmon

Since most people have to go a long way to catch salmon, here are a few tips on taking care of the catch on the way home.

Most fishing lodges and outfitters will fillet and freeze your catch, and even provide you with an insulated cardboard box to get it back home. But call ahead, and check to make sure these services are offered.

The second choice is to bring the fish back in your own soft or hard cooler. The airlines allow four pieces of luggage in the form of two check-in and two carry-on bags. Plan on counting the cooler as your second check-in, or pay the airline for one extra bag. The advantage of the soft cooler is that if you tend to pack heavy, you can stuff it inside your other check-in bags on the way there, and only pay extra on the way home.

Always bring duct tape to secure a hard cooler against leakage. The fastest way to make the airlines unhappy is to have untamed nature leaking all over the inside of their hygienic facilities.

Eating Salmon

From dark meat to light, salmon can be baked, broiled, braised, poached, grilled, or microwaved. King, sockeye, and kokanee salmon smoke and cure better, but the high oil content doesn't make them prime candidates for frying. Salmon are not as firm-fleshed as other ocean-going fish, but are much firmer than their freshwater-trout cousins and with a little care can be barbecued without falling through the grill.

The best news is that salmon is good for us, as are all fish, and doctors generally recommend two servings of fish a week, about 8 ounces (200 g), to protect against heart disease. Luckily, this is easier to do if you own a fishing rod and this cookbook.

SAINT PATRICK'S GRAVLAX WITH MUSTARD SAUCE

Yield: 1 pound (½ kg)

I was tired of corned beef and cabbage, so I decided to make this traditional Scandinavian dish with an Irish accent instead. This recipe requires no cooking, and has a short curing time, so be sure to use only fillets that have been frozen at 0°F (–17.8°C) for at least 7 days to destroy any parasites.

Saint Patrick's Gravlax with Mustard Sauce

Ingredients

1 pound (½ kg) salmon fillets, with the skin left on

⅓ cup (80 ml) salt

⅓ cup (80 ml) sugar

1 tablespoon whole pink peppercorns, crushed

3 tablespoons Irish whiskey

½ medium red onion, thinly sliced

⅔ ounce (18 g) dried dill weed, about ¼ cup (60 ml)

Preparation

1. Rinse the salmon fillets in water, pat them dry with paper towels, and wipe the fish with a small amount of oil. In a small bowl, mix together the salt, sugar, and peppercorns, and rub some of this mixture lightly on the fish. Place the fish, skin side down, in a shallow glass or plastic dish just large enough to hold it. Press the rest of the spice mixture into the fish. Spoon the whiskey over the salmon. Now lay the onion and dill weed on top.

2. Cover the bowl tightly with plastic wrap, pressing it against the fish to seal, and set the bowl in the refrigerator for 12 hours, basting three or four times with the juices. After 12 hours, turn the fish, moving the dill and onion underneath, and leave another 12 hours, basting occasionally.

3. The gravlax is ready to serve in 48 hours. Do not leave the fish in the brine for more than 48 hours, or it will get very salty. To keep it 48 hours after curing, remove it from the brine, pat it dry, and refrigerate in a sealed plastic bag.

4. To serve, discard the brine, saving 2 tablespoons for the mustard sauce, and pat the fillet dry. Lay it flat on a cutting board, and slice across the top, paper thin. Serve on toast, topped with the mustard sauce.

MUSTARD SAUCE

Ingredients

6 tablespoons country Dijon mustard

2 teaspoons mustard powder

2 tablespoons rice-wine vinegar

6 tablespoons sugar

2 tablespoons brine from the gravlax marinade

Cooking

1. In a small saucepan, combine the mustard, mustard powder, vinegar, and sugar, and bring to a boil. Stir in the brine, and beat with a spoon until the sauce is well blended and thick. You may also choose to make the sauce in the microwave.

Fly fishing (Photo © Doug Stamm)

SALMON SPREAD WITH YOGURT CHEESE

Yield: 2 cups (500 ml)

For those lucky people with a few ounces of leftover cooked salmon, here's a low-fat cracker or toast spread that fills the gaps between meals.

Ingredients

8 ounces (200 g) nonfat yogurt, about 1 cup (250 ml)
4 ounces (100 g) cooked salmon
1 tablespoon mayonnaise
2 teaspoons mustard powder
1 teaspoon dried dill weed

Preparation

1. First, reduce the yogurt to cheese: Pour the yogurt into a colander lined with several layers of cheesecloth or muslin game-bag fabric. Gather the ends of the cloth, twist a rubber band around the top, and hang the bag for 12 hours over a deep bowl. (Run a knife or pencil through the rubber band twists and lay it across the top of the bowl to hang the bag.) This will drain off the excess liquid and make the loose yogurt more the consistency of cream cheese, without the fat.

2. Combine the yogurt cheese, salmon, mayonnaise, mustard powder, and dill in a blender or food processor, and purée. Chill for 3 hours or longer. Serve the salmon spread on crackers or toast.

Salmon Spread with Yogurt Cheese

FENNEL-PICKLED SALMON

Yield: 1 pound (½ kg)

You can make the whole catch into pickled salmon, but even a pickled fish is better "fresh"—if anything pickled can be called fresh—and doesn't have a long shelf life. For larger batches of fish, multiply the recipe.

As you will notice, this recipe requires no cooking. To be safe use only fillets that have been frozen at 0°F (−17.8°C) for at least 7 days to destroy any parasites.

Fennel-Pickled Salmon

Ingredients

1 pound (½ kg) salmon fillets, with the skin left on

⅓ cup (80 ml) sugar

⅓ cup (80 ml) salt

1 tablespoon black peppercorns, coarsely crushed

2 teaspoons fennel seed, coarsely crushed

3 tablespoons sake (Japanese rice wine)

Preparation

1. Rinse the salmon fillets in water, pat them dry with paper towels, and wipe the fish with a small amount of oil. In a small bowl, combine the sugar, salt, peppercorns, and fennel. Rub the mixture on both sides of the fillets. Place the fish, skin side down, in a shallow glass or plastic dish and pour the remaining salt mixture on top. Press the mixture into the fish. Pour the sake over the fish.

2. Cover the dish tightly with plastic wrap, pressing it against the fish to seal, and place in the refrigerator for 12 hours, basting three or four times with the brine. Turn the fish over, and let it cure for another 12 hours, basting occasionally.

3. The pickled salmon is ready to serve in 48 hours. Do not leave the fish in the brine for much more than 48 hours, or it will get very salty. To keep for another 48 hours after curing, remove the fish from the brine, pat dry, and refrigerate in a sealed plastic bag.

4. To serve, remove from the brine and pat dry. Slice across the top, paper thin. Serve on crackers with cream cheese and a squeeze of lemon.

BARBECUED SALMON STEAKS WITH MANGO CHUTNEY

Yield: 8 servings

When the evenings are as hot as the tempers, and patience is at an end, fire up the barbecue for a few salmon steaks and chutney. If you can't find mangoes, substitute a cup of canned or fresh pineapple or fresh apricots.

Barbecued Salmon Steaks with Mango Chutney

Ingredients

1 mango, skinned and chopped
1 cup (250 ml) diced onion
$\frac{1}{3}$ cup (80 ml) rice vinegar
$\frac{1}{2}$ cup (125 ml) diced green bell pepper
4 figs or $\frac{1}{4}$ cup (60 ml) raisins, chopped
$\frac{1}{3}$ cup (80 ml) coarsely chopped walnuts
$\frac{1}{4}$ cup (60 ml) brown sugar
$2\frac{1}{2}$ tablespoons fresh lemon juice (about $\frac{1}{2}$ lemon)
2 teaspoons lemon zest
$\frac{1}{2}$ teaspoon mustard powder
$\frac{1}{4}$ teaspoon curry powder
8 salmon steaks, 1 inch ($2\frac{1}{2}$ cm) thick

Cooking

1. To make the mango chutney, combine all the ingredients except the salmon in a medium saucepan over high heat, and bring to a low boil. Reduce the heat to simmer, cover, and cook for 30 minutes, stirring occasionally to make sure it doesn't stick. Set aside, until the chutney cools to room temperature.

2. Start four dozen briquettes or preheat the propane barbecue on high for 10 minutes. When the briquettes are white hot, or the propane barbecue heated and turned down to medium heat, remove the rack and spray or brush with a light coating of oil; this will prevent the steaks from sticking. Grill the steaks about 5 minutes to a side or until flaky but moist. Serve each steak with a generous spoonful or two of the mango chutney.

CHILLED BARBECUED SALMON STEAKS WITH FENNEL SALSA

Yield: 6–8 servings

Since this is a chilled salad, barbecue these steaks early in the day, or next time you barbecue salmon steaks, cook up enough for one additional meal, and stick the extra steaks in the refrigerator. The next night, you'll be eating delicious salmon, and salsa with a new attitude. It's guaranteed to cool you off.

Ingredients

⅔ cup (160 ml) chopped fresh fennel, including the root, stalks, and leaves
⅔ cup (160 ml) onion
1 cup (250 ml) very ripe tomato
½ jalapeño pepper, seeds and stem removed
¼ teaspoon salt
8 salmon steaks, 1 inch (2½ cm) thick

Preparation

1. One to two hours before eating, start four dozen charcoal briquettes, or preheat the propane barbecue. When the coals are white hot, or the propane barbecue is ready to turn down to medium. Remove the grate and lightly brush or spray it with oil to prevent sticking. Grill the steaks about 5 minutes to a side or until the flesh flakes easily with a fork but is still moist. Chill 1–2 hours.

2. To make the salsa, combine the fennel, onion, tomato, jalapeño, and salt in a food processor and blend 3–5 seconds, until the salsa is chopped but not puréed. Let the salsa cool 30 minutes at room temperature, then chill 1 hour with the salmon. Serve salmon steaks topped by a generous portion of fennel salsa and accompanied by fresh potato salad.

Chilled Barbecued Salmon Steaks with Fennel Salsa

BRAISED SALMON STEAKS

Yield: 6 servings

Chinook salmon (Photo © Doug Stamm)

Salmon steaks are always quick and easy to fix, but braising provides more moisture to the cooking process. The spices in this braising recipe provide lots of flavor—and if you happen to be a mushroom collector, wild mushrooms are a wonderful addition.

Ingredients

1 cup (250 ml) dry white wine

¼ cup (60 ml) fresh lemon juice (about 1 lemon)

8 ounces (250 g) mushrooms, sliced, about 3 cups (750 ml)

½ small yellow onion, finely chopped

¼ teaspoon salt

6 tablespoons margarine, softened

1 teaspoon crushed dried tarragon

2 tablespoons chopped green onions, greens only

6 salmon steaks

Cooking

1. Combine the wine and lemon juice in a glass bowl, and marinate the mushrooms in the mixture about 30 minutes. In a separate bowl, combine the onion, salt, margarine, tarragon, and green onions, and mix gently with a spoon.

2. In a large skillet, brown the steaks in 3 tablespoons of the margarine mixture.

3. Add the rest of the seasoned margarine, the mushrooms and their marinade to the pan. Cover and simmer for 15 minutes. Serve the steaks with the mushroom sauce spooned over the top, accompanied by salad and fresh, steamed asparagus topped by a grating of Parmesan cheese.

Note: If you have trouble getting dry white wines where you live, as I do, substitute extra-dry vermouth. It's readily available.

OVEN-BROILED SALMON FILLETS WITH WORCESTERSHIRE-AND-BUTTER BASTE

Yield: 4 servings

Indoor broiling is a no-frills way to get a delicious dinner in little time. Turn the oven to broil, let it preheat for 10 minutes with the door closed, and you're ready to go. The best fillets for grilling are ¾–1 inch (2–2 ½ cm) at the thickest part. Anything thinner will fall apart or dry out during cooking; if they are much thicker, they will not grill properly.

Fishing for that secret hole below a dock (Photo © Doug Stamm)

Ingredients

3 tablespoons butter or margarine
1 teaspoon Worcestershire sauce
2 tablespoons fresh lemon juice
3–4 drops red pepper Tabasco sauce
1 pound (½ kg) salmon fillet, with the skin left on

Cooking

1. In a small saucepan, bring all the ingredients except the fillets to a low boil. Turn the heat down and simmer 15 minutes. You may also choose to microwave the sauce.

2. Preheat the broiler and broiler rack, then remove the rack and lightly brush or spray with oil. Place the steaks skin side down on the rack and grill them about 3–4 minutes to a side. Baste each side with the Worcestershire butter several times. The fish is done when you insert a fork, twist gently, and the flesh flakes easily, and is still moist.

BARBECUED SALMON FILLETS WITH FAN POTATOES AND DILL BUTTER

Yield: 4 servings

Grilling skinned fillets creates a logistical problem: How to turn the delicate, half-cooked flesh without having it fall into the abyss. There are two easy options. The first is to cut a length of aluminum foil, perforate the surface with a fork in several places, and lay the fillet on that. This keeps dinner out of the coals. The second choice makes life even easier. Purchase a wonderful invention known as a hinged grate, and lay the fish inside. The advantage of the grate is that you eliminate the problem of having the fillet fall apart when you turn it, and you still can brush with oil or marinade through the wire mesh. Of course some people don't bother to turn fillets at all. The fish is still cooked, but it's simply not the same.

Ingredients

4 baking potatoes, skinned
$\frac{1}{4}$ cup (60 ml) butter or margarine
1 teaspoon dried dill weed
1 pound ($\frac{1}{2}$ kg) salmon fillet, skinned

Cooking

1. Place a skinned potato in a large spoon, and cut across the width of the potato, almost all the way through, every $\frac{1}{4}$ inch, creating a fanned potato for faster baking. Place the potatoes in a pie pan or on a baking sheet. Preheat the oven to 350°F (175°C).

2. In a small saucepan, melt the butter, add the dill, and stir well. You may also choose to make the dill butter in the microwave. Pour half of the butter mixture over the fanned potatoes, and bake 45–60 minutes until they are fork tender.

3. Preheat the propane barbecue, or start four dozen briquettes. When the briquettes are white hot, or the propane unit ready and turned down to medium, place the fillet in a hinged grate or on perforated foil. Grill about 3–4 minutes per side, brushing the remaining dill butter over the fillet several times while cooking. The fillet is done when you can twist gently with a fork at the thickest part, and the fish flakes, but is still moist.

BAKED WHOLE SALMON

Yield: 4–6 servings

A 4-pound (2 kg) salmon, live weight, is just about perfect for baking—primarily because it will fit in the oven easily. Cleaned, the fish yields about 2½ pounds (1¼ kg) of meat. That makes an easy chore of feeding a crowd, and baking is one of the easiest ways to cook salmon.

Fishing in the Bangor salmon pool, Penobscot River, Maine (Photo © Thomas Mark Szelog)

Ingredients

1 salmon, 2 ½ pounds (1 ¼ kg), whole
Salt and pepper, to taste
2 tablespoons Madeira wine
1 teaspoon mustard powder
4–5 thin slices of onion

Cooking

1. Preheat oven to 400°F (205°C). Lay out a 2-foot (60-cm) length of aluminum foil on the counter. Rinse the fish in cold water and pat it dry with paper towels. Set the fish on the foil. Season the inside of the fish with salt and pepper. In a small bowl, combine the Madeira and mustard powder, stir until the powder dissolves, and pour the mixture inside the fish. Lay the onion slices inside as well.

2. Seal the salmon in the foil and place in a shallow baking pan or cookie sheet. Bake for 45 minutes. Remove the fish from the oven and poke a meat thermometer through the foil into the thickest part of the fish. Wait 10 minutes, then check the temperature. The fish is done when the thermometer reads 135°F (57°C).

Note: It's the last 5–10°F (2.75–5.5°C) degrees of cooking that are the quickest. So, if you test the salmon and the thermometer reads 120–130°F (49–54°C), continue baking with caution. It's not a logical progression: If it took 45 minutes to reach 120°F (49°C), or about 2⅓ minutes of cooking per 1°F (0.5°C), you would think it will take another 10 minutes to reach 135°F (57°C). But in 10 minutes, the salmon will be toast. Go cautiously those last minutes of cooking; and remember that whatever temperature the thermometer reads, it will creep up about 10°F (5.5°C) if you let the salmon sit out of the oven for 10 minutes.

Fᴀᴛ Sᴀʟᴍᴏɴ Mᴏᴜssᴇ

Yield: 4 servings

A baked whole salmon is a lot of food for a family of two like mine. So rather than let it suffer the fate of so many Christmas turkeys, we make mousse, usually the Skinny Salmon Mousse recipe that follows, but for special occasions, we make it fat and happy.

Fat Salmon Mousse

Ingredients

½ cup (125 ml) clam juice

1 envelope (1 tablespoon) unflavored gelatin

8 ounces (200 g) cooked salmon

2 teaspoons anchovy paste

2 teaspoons capers

1 green onion

3 tablespoons fresh lemon juice (about
¾ lemon)

½ teaspoon dried leaf tarragon

½ cup (125 ml) sour cream

¾ cup (185 ml) mayonnaise

10 drops red pepper Tabasco sauce

Preparation

1. Pour the clam juice into a saucepan and sprinkle the gelatin on top. Let it sit until the gelatin crystals have softened. Heat the mixture over low heat and stir until the gelatin is dissolved. Remove the pan from the heat and let the juice cool to room temperature, about 10 minutes.

2. Once the gelatin has cooled, combine it with the rest of the ingredients in a blender or food processor and purée.

3. Pour into a lightly oiled 4-cup (1-liter) mousse mold or loaf pan. Chill until set, about 8 hours. The light coating of oil should let the mousse slip easily from the mold; if not, dip it in warm water a few seconds then invert carefully onto a platter. Serve with summer garden salad and garlic toast.

SKINNY SALMON MOUSSE

Yield: 4 servings

Here's the good half of that evil twin Fat Salmon Mousse. But while it's light enough to make often, it's still full of flavor.

Ingredients

1 envelope (1 tablespoon) unflavored gelatin
½ cup (125 ml) water
2 tablespoons chopped onion
2 tablespoons fresh lemon juice (about ½ lemon)
1 cup (250 ml) nonfat yogurt
8 ounces (200 g) cooked salmon
½ jalapeño pepper, seed and stems removed
1 teaspoon green jalapeño Tabasco sauce
½ teaspoon ground cumin
¼ teaspoon chili powder
¼ teaspoon salt
⅛ teaspoon pepper

Preparation

1. Sprinkle the gelatin over the water in a saucepan, and let sit until the gelatin softens. Heat the mixture over low heat and stir till the gelatin crystals dissolve. Let cool to room temperature, about 10 minutes.

2. Combine the gelatin, onion, lemon juice, and yogurt in a blender or food processor and blend at high speed about 20 seconds. Add the remaining ingredients and blend another 20 seconds at high speed until everything is puréed.

3. Pour into a lightly oiled 4-cup (1-liter) mousse mold or loaf pan. Chill until firm, about 8 hours. Turn out carefully onto a platter. If the light coating of oil doesn't make the mold slick enough, dip the mold in warm water about 10 seconds, then turn out. Serve on crackers.

Drift fishing on the Yellowstone River, Montana (Photo © George Wuerthner)

Barbecued Whole Steelhead with Hot Paprika Sauce

Yield: 6–8 servings

Barbecuing is an excellent way to prepare distinctively flavored fish like steelhead. The smoke flavor adds a little something to the pot, without completely overwhelming the essential character of this fish, as it would with more delicate varieties. This is also a great way to get out of the kitchen.

Ingredients

1 steelhead, 4 pounds (2 kg), whole
Salt and pepper, to taste
2 ounces (50 g) or $\frac{1}{2}$ cup (125 ml) red table grapes
$\frac{1}{4}$ cup (125 ml) butter or margarine, melted

Cooking

1. Preheat the propane barbecue on high, or start four dozen charcoal briquettes. Rinse the fish inside and out, and pat dry with paper towels. Season lightly with the salt and pepper, and tuck the grapes into the body cavity. Make an aluminum-foil "grilling liner" for the steelhead: Use heavy-duty foil, double thickness, and three or four times the width of the fish. Lay the steelhead on one side of the liner. Halfway through cooking, you'll fold the fish onto the other side.

2. When the coals are white hot, or the propane unit preheated and reduced to medium, place the fish with its foil liner on the grill. Insert a meat thermometer into the thickest part of the fish, and close the grill top. Brush occasionally with the melted butter. Cook the steelhead about 8–10 minutes for each 1 inch $(2\frac{1}{2}$ cm) of thickness. About halfway through cooking, fold the fish and foil over on the second side. The fish is done when the meat thermometer reaches 135°F (57°C).

3. To serve, lift off the top layer of skin, slide a spatula between the flesh and ribs, and lift off the top fillet. Remove the backbone (and the head, if necessary), and lift the other fillet off the skin on bottom. Serve with the hot paprika sauce, potato salad, roasted corn, and apple pie.

Note: It's the last 5–10°F (2.75–5.5°C) degrees of cooking that are the quickest. So, if you test the salmon and the thermometer reads 120–130°F (49–54°C), continue baking with caution. It's not a logical progression: If it took 45 minutes to reach 120°F (49°C), or about $2\frac{1}{3}$ minutes of cooking per 1°F (0.5°C), you would think it will take another 10 minutes to reach 135°F (57°C). But in 10 minutes, the salmon will be toast. Go cautiously those last minutes of cooking; and remember that whatever temperature the thermometer reads, it will creep up about 10°F (5.5°C) if you let the salmon sit out of the oven for 10 minutes.

HOT PAPRIKA SAUCE

Ingredients

3 tablespoons butter or margarine

1 tablespoon hot paprika

$\frac{1}{4}$ cup (60 ml) dry white wine or extra-dry vermouth

$\frac{1}{2}$ cup (125 ml) sour cream

Cooking

1. Melt the butter in small saucepan. Add the paprika and stir over medium heat until well mixed. Add the white wine, and cook until the sauce is smooth. Remove from heat, and stir the sour cream into the sauce. Serve immediately or chill.

Note: In Montana, hot paprika is a rare and sometime thing. I generally have to buy it from a mail-order spice house located in bratwurst country. That's what hot paprika is usually used for, I hear. Above all, don't substitute sweet Hungarian paprika. In a pinch, 1 teaspoon of chili powder will taste almost as good.

Fishing in Tanada Lake, Wrangell–St. Elias National Park, Alaska (Photo © George Wuerthner)

BARBECUED STEELHEAD FILLETS WITH RÉMOULADE

Yield: 3–4 servings

Fishing for Steelhead (Photo © Erwin and Peggy Bauer)

One easy way to handle fillets on the barbecue is to double-skewer them with wooden skewers. Simply put, lay the steelhead fillets on a cutting board and run one skewer up one side of the fillet, a second up the other side. It works best if the skewers are set at an angle; lower ends further apart than the uppers, like an easel. This method keeps the fish from falling apart, and if you soak the skewers in water 30 minutes before cooking, they won't scorch. The rémoulade is a reward for not dropping the fillets into the coals.

Ingredients

1 cup (250 ml) mayonnaise
1 clove garlic
½ teaspoon dried tarragon
½ teaspoon dried mustard
1 hard-boiled egg
2 teaspoons capers
1 tablespoon fresh parsley
½ teaspoon anchovy paste
1 pound (½ kg) steelhead fillet, cut into
    serving sizes

Cooking

1. To make the rémoulade, combine all of the ingredients except the fillets in a food processor or blender, and purée. Chill the rémoulade at least 1 hour before serving.

2. Preheat the propane barbecue, or start three dozen charcoal briquettes. When the propane unit is preheated and turned down to medium, or the briquettes are white hot, lay the skewered fillets on a piece of lightly oiled foil on the barbecue grate. With a knife, poke holes in the foil. Close the cover and let the fish cook until the fillets are translucent and flake easily: 6–8 minutes for fillets less than 1 inch (2½ cm) thick; 10–15 minutes for fillets 1–1½ inch (2½–3½ cm) thick. Serve immediately with lots of rémoulade and a selection of raw, fresh vegetables, such as carrots, radishes, cucumbers, broccoli florets, and sugar pea pods.

POACHED SALMON WITH CORIANDER SAUCE

Yield: 4–6 servings

Poaching is an excellent way to cook whole fish or fillets without adding any more fat. A true poaching pan is the perfect long, narrow shape for fish, and comes with a removable cooking platform to lift the cooked fish out in one piece. But if you don't own a poacher, any large covered roaster will do; just wrap the fish in cheesecloth before you cook it. With a little care, you'll still have a whole fish to serve for Sunday dinner.

Fish Ingredients

1 onion, sliced
1 carrot, sliced
1 tablespoon crushed dried basil
2 bay leaves
1 cup (250 ml) minced fresh parsley
3 cloves garlic
1 ½ teaspoons whole peppercorns
1 teaspoon salt
3 tablespoons red wine vinegar
1 salmon, 2 ½ pounds (1 ¼ kg), whole

Coriander Sauce Ingredients

3 tablespoons butter or margarine
3 tablespoons flour
½ cup (125 ml) poaching liquid, reserved and cooled to room temperature
1 cup (250 ml) milk
¼ teaspoon salt
¼ teaspoon black pepper
1 teaspoon ground coriander

Cooking the Fish

1. In a fish poacher or roaster large enough to lay the salmon on its side, combine all the cooking ingredients except the fish. Add enough water to the pan to cover the thickness of the fish, then remove the fish. Bring the mixture to a boil, reduce the heat, and simmer for 15 minutes.

2. Place the fish in the pan and set your timer once when the water returns to a simmer. Do not boil the fish—it will break up. Allow 10 minutes for each 1 inch (2 ½ cm) of thickness for fresh fish. Lift the salmon from the cooking liquid, and serve hot with the coriander sauce. (Reserve ½ cup/125 ml poaching liquid for the sauce.)

Cooking the Sauce

Melt the butter on medium heat in a small saucepan, add the flour, and cook until well mixed. Add the reserved poaching liquid and stir until smooth. Gradually add the milk, and continue cooking till the sauce is thick. Add the salt, pepper, and coriander, and stir to blend.

Note: While the fish poaches, it is important to keep the water just below a bubbling boil. A bubbling boil will cause the fish to fall apart, and alter the cooking time. The other important thing is to take the fish out of the cooking liquid as soon as the fish is done. Do not let the fish cool in the pot; it will be overdone and tough.

SALMON *MINESTRA*

Yield: 4–6 servings

Minestra is an oven soup, which means you cut up the ingredients, throw them in the pot, and let the oven do the work. If you're working around the house, or going out for a couple of hours of fishing, it's the easiest way I know to have supper waiting for you.

Ingredients

1 ½ pounds (¾ kg) potatoes, diced
1 red onion, sliced
1 sweet green bell pepper, sliced
4 cloves garlic, minced
1 bay leaf
1 can diced tomatoes, 28 ounces (795 g)
½ cup (125 ml) sake (Japanese rice wine) or dry white wine
¼ teaspoon ground turmeric
¼ teaspoon dried leaf thyme
½ teaspoon mustard powder
1 ½ teaspoons salt

1 cup (250 ml) fish stock (see page 74), or 1 cup (250 ml) clam juice
2 pounds (1 kg) salmon chunks
1 tablespoon orange zest
1 tablespoon lemon zest

Cooking

1. Preheat the oven to 400°F (205°C). Combine all the ingredients in a 4-quart (3 ½ -liter) Dutch oven, stir, cover, and place in the oven. Cook for 30 minutes, then turn the oven down to 350°F (175°C) and cook another 60 minutes. Serve with sourdough rolls.

Sockeye salmon (Photo © John Barsness)

STUFFED WHOLE STEELHEAD

Yield: 6 servings

Whole fish up to 6 pounds (3 kg) are ideal for baking, and since salmon and steelhead have a variety of crustaceans in their diets, it only seems logical to add a little shrimp to this stuffing.

Ingredients

1 steelhead, 3 pounds (1½ kg), whole
½ cup (125 ml) diced onion
1 stalk celery, diced
3 tablespoons butter
4 ounces (100 g) shrimp, cleaned and diced
1 teaspoon dried thyme leaves
2 cups (500 ml) dried bread cubes
2 tablespoons Madeira wine
½ cup (125 ml) fish stock or chicken broth

Cooking

1. Wash the fish inside and out, then pat dry with paper towels. Preheat the oven to 450°F (235°C).
2. To make the stuffing, sauté the onions and celery in butter in a large skillet until the vegetables are soft. Add the shrimp and thyme. Continue cooking until the shrimp turn pink. Add the bread cubes and toss in the vegetable mixture, adding the Madeira and then the broth to moisten the mixture.
3. Stuff the fish with the bread crumb–shrimp mixture. Using toothpicks as skewers, tie the body cavity closed with light twine. Lay the fish in a lightly oiled pan, and oil the surface of the fish. Now, measure the thickness of the fish, and bake 10 minutes for each 1 inch (2½ cm) of thickness. The fish is done when a meat thermometer reads 135°F (57°C), or when the flesh in the thickest part is just slightly translucent and flakes when a fork is inserted and twisted gently.
4. Remove the stuffing. Pull off the top layer of the fish's skin, sliding a spatula between the top fillet and ribcage, and lift the fillet off. Remove the backbone and lift the second fillet off the bottom skin. Serve the fish and stuffing accompanied by lemon wedges.

Note: It's the last 5–10°F (2.75–5.5°C) degrees of cooking that are the quickest. So, if you test the salmon and the thermometer reads 120–130°F (49–54°C), continue baking with caution. It's not a logical progression: If it took 45 minutes to reach 120°F (49°C), or about 2⅓ minutes of cooking per 1°F (0.5°C), you would think it will take another 10 minutes to reach 135°F (57°C). But in 10 minutes, the salmon will be toast. Go cautiously those last minutes of cooking; and remember that whatever temperature the thermometer reads, it will creep up about 10°F (5.5°C) if you let the salmon sit out of the oven for 10 minutes.

GENERAL RULES FOR SMOKING SALMON

Use only fresh fish, or fish frozen immediately after catching. While most fish can be smoked, fattier varieties like salmon and trout are best. The fat absorbs more of the smoky flavors, while keeping the flesh moist. Leaving the skin on also helps keep the flesh moist and makes the cooked fish easier to handle.

Use dry wood—no bark and no evergreens. The sap from evergreens will leave a bitter flavor. Alderwood, mesquite, hickory, and most fruit tree woods, like apple, cherry, and peach, add a lot of flavor to the fish. Fruit trees add a sweet, mellow flavor; alder is the favorite among some for salmon. Many of these woods are available commercially.

Check the temperature of your smoker. The easiest way to do this is to attach a wire to an oven thermometer, then run the wire up through the vent, with the thermometer hanging over the food. Check the temperature first after 15 minutes of preheating, then again when you believe the fish to be half cooked. Check the fish that second time to see how well done it is, and refigure the final cooking time. As always, thicker cuts will take longer than thinner ones. The cooking time in these recipes are based on a temperature of 140–150°F (60–65°C), as in my electric smoker.

The fish is done when it is opaque, pulls away from the skin easily, and still looks moist. Whether smoking, frying, baking, or grilling, if the fish looks, smells, and tastes cooked, it *is* cooked. If you are unfamiliar with the smoker, or smoking in general, check the fish often, every 1–2 hours; when it's close to being done, check more often.

Once the fish is smoked, cool it down to room temperature and serve immediately, or wrap in resealable plastic bags. It will keep in the refrigerator for 4 weeks, or in the freezer 3–6 months.

The following two recipes are just two variations for smoking fish. Start with 2–4 cups (500–1000 ml) of water, ½ cup (125 ml) salt, and ½–1 cup (125–250 ml) sugar for each 1 pound (500 g) of fish—then add any seasoning you want, from Italian to Mexican, Greek to Chinese, hot peppers or cool dill, or even the sweet flavor of maple syrup. The fish is like a baked potato you can add anything to.

Fly fishing in a channel of the Snake River, Grand Teton National Park (Photo © Erwin and Peggy Bauer)

PEPPER-SMOKED SALMON

Yield: 1 pound ($\frac{1}{2}$ kg)

People have been smoking salmon for a long time, but since the invention of the electric smoker, it's gotten a lot easier to control the temperature and ensure a predictable outcome. Here are two recipes, variations on the basic sugar-and-salt solution, with an invitation to experiment. Start with good, fresh fish, though; the results are only as good as the ingredients.

Ingredients

2 cups (500 ml) hot water
1 cup (250 ml) brown sugar
$\frac{1}{2}$ cup (125 ml) coarse salt
$\frac{1}{4}$ teaspoon red pepper flakes
$\frac{1}{4}$ teaspoon cumin seeds, crushed
1 pound ($\frac{1}{2}$ kg) salmon fillet

Preparation

1. To make the brine, combine the water, sugar, salt, pepper flakes, and cumin seeds in a bowl. Stir the ingredients until fully dissolved and let cool to room temperature.

2. In the meantime, rinse the fillet and pat it dry with a paper towel. Place it in a non-corrosive dish that is small enough to hold the fish completely submerged in the brine. If necessary, cut the fillet to fit your bowl but keep it to a single layer. When the brine has cooled, pour it over the fish, cover, and refrigerate 12 hours, turning occasionally.

3. Remove the fillets from the brine, rinse gently, and pat dry with paper towels. Allow to air dry at room temperature on a cooling rack for 1–2 hours until the flesh is tacky to the touch. The fillets are now ready to smoke.

Smoking

1. For an electric smoker, soak your wood chips in the smoking pan for 30 minutes, then drain off the excess water before using. Place the chip pan in the smoker, turn the smoker on, and wait for the first sign of smoke to come out the top; in other words, preheat the smoker. When the smoker is ready, place the fish on the shelves, leaving 1–2 inches ($2\frac{1}{2}$–5 cm) of space between the fish fillets to allow the smoke to circulate. After about an hour, check the chip pan, and add more chips; refill the pan again when the last is reduced to ashes, after about one hour. Three chip pans will give you a rich, smoky flavor.

1. Cook until the fish is opaque throughout, about 8–10 hours at 140–150°F (60–65°C). Ambient air temperature plays a role in how long the fish needs to smoke: on a 55°F (13°C) day, it takes 9 hours; cooler days will take longer, and warmer days will require less time.

3. Serve immediately with crackers, or store for later. See the general directions for smoking for specifics of storage.

SOY-SMOKED SALMON

Yield: 1 pound (½ kg)

Ginger has always been one of my favorite flavors, so eventually it ended up in a brine. The soy sauce adds more smoke and power to the flavor, as well as sodium, so I've cut down on the table salt to make room for it.

Ingredients

1 quart (1 liter) hot water
¼ cup (60 ml) coarse salt
½ cup (125 ml) sugar
2 teaspoons crystallized ginger
¼ cup (60 ml) soy sauce
1 pound (½ kg) salmon fillets

Preparation

1. To make the brine, combine all the ingredients except the fillets in a blender, purée, and let cool to room temperature.

2. In the meantime, rinse the fillet and pat dry with a paper towel. Place it in a single layer in a non-corrosive dish that is small enough to hold the fish completely submerged in the brine. When the brine has cooled, pour it over the fillets, cover, and refrigerate 12 hours, turning occasionally.

3. Remove the fillets from the brine, rinse gently, and pat dry with paper towels. Allow the fillets to air dry at room temperature on a cooling rack for 1–2 hours until the flesh is tacky to the touch. The fillets are now ready to smoke.

Smoking

1. For an electric smoker, soak your wood chips in the smoking pan for 30 minutes, then drain off the excess liquid before using. Place the chip pan in the smoker, turn the smoker on, and wait 15 minutes, or until the first sign of smoke appears; in other words, preheat the smoker. When the smoker is ready, place the fish on the shelves, leaving 1–2 inches (2½–5 cm) space between the shelves to allow the smoke to circulate. After about an hour, check the chip pan, and add more chips; refill the pan again when the last is reduced to ashes, after about hour. Three pans will give you a rich, smoky flavor.

2. Cook until the fish is opaque throughout, about 8–10 hours at 140–150°F (60–65°C). Ambient air temperature plays a role in how long the fish needs to smoke: on a 55°F (13°C) day, it takes 9 hours; cooler days will take longer, and warmer days will require less time.

3. Serve immediately with crackers, or store for later. See the general directions for smoking for specifics of storage.

TROUT

While there are some days of salmon fishing that leave the arms leaden and tired, and your heart wishing the fish simply wouldn't bite again, though you don't have the sense to stop casting, trout fishing is usually a more delicate affair. Whether you fish the rainbow spawn in spring, the brown run in the fall, naive brookies in tiny, overgrown streams, or gaudy cutthroats in high mountain lakes, the tug on the line is more a call to attention than to action, and all trout have their own allure. They all leave us hungry for more, and the most difficult question we face as anglers is which trout and where, with what tackle and rod, and how much time we can steal from work, home, and family to chase the wily trout. And while it is fun to catch a trout, it is as much fun to eat one. No matter how you catch them, all trout are easy to cook, and all trout taste good.

In this world of quantifying everything, however, let's get a few things straight. Rainbows are universally held to be the most fun to catch and, therefore, the most frequently stocked, while brook trout are renowned far and wide as the best to eat.

Which brings us, briefly, to the science of trout. Brookies are technically a char, less closely related to rainbows and browns than they are to Arctic char, lake trout, and Dolly Varden. And all chars are generally considered the best "trout" to eat. They all tend to have more orange flesh than true trout, such as rainbows and browns, and their flesh is closer to the color of salmon. (Which brings us back to that poor Atlantic salmon: It had three strikes against it. It lived in heavily populated areas, it jumped like a rainbow, and it had delicious, deep-orange flesh.)

Rainbows that live in lakes with freshwater shrimp develop this orange flesh, too. Despite my own preference for small streams and naive fish, there was a small agricultural-irrigation lake we used to fish, where rainbow fingerlings were stocked, and two years later, were caught as 15-inch ($37\frac{1}{2}$-cm) "belly" trout: fat, deep-orange-fleshed fish that you had to hold against your belly to unhook. They had that richer, more intense flavor, that all char have: brookies, Dolly Varden, lake trout, and Arctic char, as well as other trout that are just lucky enough to have scuds in their diet. But don't turn down a white-fleshed trout; they are good eating, too.

Around our house, we tend to catch trout in the places we like to fish, and we cook them immediately. The key factor for us is how many people we want to feed, therefore, how many fish do we need for dinner. The principle then is to keep the first fish keep any damaged fish, and if you are really pressed for time, hit only the hot spots and keep everything you hook. Once, we caught dinner for four in less than 15 minutes—that included rigging, walking the 30 yards from truck to stream, and arguing briefly over who would get the first cast.

Cooking Trout

Trout come in different sizes; when you are ready to cook, you will want to keep in mind some general guidelines based on the size of the fish you carry to the kitchen, backyard barbecue, or campfire. The first thing to remember is that crappies aren't the only panfish; trout come panfish-size, too. The second thing to remember is not to cheat on the size of your pan.

A pan-sized fish is any fish up to 14 inches (35 cm) in length, meaning that you can fit it in a standard 9-inch (22-cm) frying pan. Traditionally, a pan-sized fish is fried with the head and tail on, although that's not a necessity. Some people like this method of cooking so well, they cut a fish in half to fit the pan-size requirement; others simply remove the head to make a bit more room. Remember, however, that the cheek of any fish and the tail of those fried are considered delicacies.

The ideal size to pan fry a trout is 6–8 inches (15–20 cm), because they will cook quickly inside without burning the coating. A 10-inch (25-cm) trout has to be propped up on it's back against the side of the pan to finish cooking the meatiest part of the fish without overcooking the rest of it.

Medium-sized trout are 14–20 inches (35–50 cm) in length and are too small for making steaks, but you can do anything else you want with them—bake, fry, poach, grill, broil, or barbecue, fillet the fish, or cook it whole.

Large trout are 20 inches and more in length (50+ cm). A fish this large is like a small salmon, and unless it's really skinny, you can steak it out. To be sure, measure the fish through the thickest part, first laying it on its side: the fish should be a minimum of $2\frac{1}{2}$ inches ($6\frac{1}{2}$ cm) deep to provide you with a good-sized steak.

Larger fish generally have a higher fat content, so you need to cook them with methods that get the oil out. Barbecuing, grilling, poaching, broiling, and brais-

Previous page: Rainbow trout (Photo © Doug Stamm)

ing are excellent methods. Fatty fish are also ideal for smoking and salt curing, as in gravlax. But don't fry these large, oily fish; you'll get better results with these other methods.

As a rule, trout don't need to be boned or scaled. In fact, with trout 6 inches (15 cm) or less in length, the bones are soft enough to eat. Canning dissolves bones. Smoking makes bones stick out like a sore thumb, and obliging your guests to pick around the bones makes this delicacy last longer.

With larger fish, it is much easier to peel the meat off the bones after cooking. For instance, to serve a whole fish, remove it carefully from the grill or pot, and lay it out on a cutting board. Peel the skin off the top, and with a spatula or two, lift the top fillet off the back bone. Now, remove the backbone, then lift the second fillet off the bottom skin, and it's boned.

If you prefer to remove the bones before cooking, here's a slick method. Begin by cleaning the fish and extending the opening from the vent to the tail, then cut off the head. Lay the fish belly-up on a cutting board. With a sharp scissors, cut through the rib bones as close to the spine as you can. Now, lift the spine off the fish, using a sharp knife to free it from the meat. Slide the knife under the cut end of the rib bones, and lift them off. Run your fingers over the flesh to make sure you got all the bones, then cook your favorite recipe. I have used boned fish in pickling recipes; without the bones, the trout go into the jar much more easily.

As usual, it's a matter of taste. If you want a little-bitty 1-inch (3-cm) steak, go for it. If you like frying oily fish, have at it. And if you want to spend hours pulling every little bone out of every little fish, I'm happy for you. Personally, I'd rather go fishing.

Fly fishing (Photo © Doug Stamm)

PINK TROUT

Yield: 4–6 servings

Pink Trout

The best-tasting lake trout come in at under 6 pounds (3 kg), and fortunately, a 6-pound lake trout makes into very healthy fillets. You can also use 2 pounds (1 kg) of whole, smaller trout.

Ingredients

1 medium onion, sliced thin
½ teaspoon salt
¼ teaspoon black pepper
½ teaspoon crushed red pepper (more to taste)
4 tablespoons butter or margarine

2 pounds (1 kg) lake trout fillet, or 2 whole trout, 16 inches (40 cm) long each
1 can unsweetened coconut milk, 14 ounces (400 g)
2 ripe roma or plum tomatoes, diced
2 tablespoons tomato paste

Fly fishing in the Platte River Canyon, Colorado (Photo © R.E. Barber)

Cooking

1. In a large skillet over medium heat, sauté the onions with salt, black pepper, and crushed red peppers in the butter.

2. Cut the fillets into individual servings, pat dry with paper towels, and sauté in the onion mixture until just opaque. Remove the fillets.

Add the coconut milk, tomatoes, and paste to the skillet, cover, and simmer gently about 15 minutes, stirring often until the sauce is thickened. To serve, lay the fish on a platter and cover with the sauce. Serve with fresh garden salad and mashed potatoes made with half sweet potatoes and half white potatoes.

BAKED LAKE TROUT FILLETS WITH CRUMBY WINE

Yield: 4–6 servings

Baking is one of the easiest ways to cook fish, and searing the trout first retains a lot of the flavor. Choose a smaller lake trout, under 6 pounds (3 kg), for the best-tasting results. Larger fish can be more fun to land, but they have a muddy flavor. Take their snapshot and let them go.

Ingredients

1 cup (250 ml) dried bread crumbs
1 teaspoon dried leaf thyme
4 cloves garlic, minced
1 teaspoon lemon zest
1 teaspoon black pepper
1½ pounds (¾ kg) trout fillets
2 tablespoons peanut or canola oil
½ cup (125 ml) dry white wine or extra-dry vermouth

Cooking

1. In a small bowl, combine the bread crumbs, thyme, garlic, and lemon zest. Toss and season with the pepper. Preheat the oven to 425°F (220°C). Lightly oil a baking dish.

2. Cut the fillets into individual serving sizes, and pat dry with paper towels. Heat the oil in a large skillet on medium-high heat until the oil just begins to smoke. Sear the fillets quickly, on one side only, and transfer to the lightly oiled baking dish, seared side up. Gently pour the wine over the fillets, then sprinkle with the seasoned bread crumb mixture.

3. Bake 5–7 minutes, or until the fillets are opaque. Serve immediately with mashed Parmesan potatoes: 6 cups (1,500 ml) potatoes mashed with milk and ¼ cup (60 ml) grated Parmesan cheese.

Dolly Varden (Photo © John Barsness)

SCALLOP-STUFFED LAKE TROUT

Yield: 4–6 servings

Here's a stuffing to serve Easter Sunday, if you're fortunate enough to have a freshly caught fish. A frozen fish is a good substitute as long as it was frozen within a few hours after being caught. Trout are not as refrigerator friendly as walleye, pike, bass, and other warmer-water fish. Those fish can cool their heels in the refrigerator a couple of days, and you'll still have a good dinner. But trout, including lake trout, will suffer.

Ingredients

1 lake trout, 3–4 pounds (1½–2 kg), whole
1 tablespoon oil
½ teaspoon salt
½ teaspoon pepper
1 onion, chopped
4 ounces (100g) uncooked scallops, diced, about ½ cup (125 ml)
4 ounces (100 g) fresh mushrooms, sliced, about 1½ cups (375 ml)
3 tablespoon fresh lemon juice
3 tablespoons extra-dry vermouth
1½ teaspoons dried leaf oregano

Cooking

1. Preheat the oven to 400°F (205°C). Rinse the trout gently and pat dry inside and out with paper towels. Now rub the fish inside and out with oil. Season inside and out with salt and pepper, and place in a lightly oiled baking dish. In a small bowl, combine the onion, raw scallops, and mushrooms, toss, and stuff loosely into the fish. Combine the lemon juice, vermouth, and oregano and pour over the fish and into the stuffing.

2. Cover the baking dish with foil and bake about 10 minutes per 1 inch (2½ cm) of thickness, measured after the fish was stuffed and laying on its side. The fish is done when the skin peels away easily. Serve with lemon wedges, wild rice, and steamed, fresh broccoli.

Lemon-Pickled Trout

Yield: 1 quart (1 liter)

Lemon-Pickled Trout

All you really need in order to pickle a trout is a jar of vinegar, but what would life be without variety? With Norwegians for in-laws, I've learned there's no end to the possible ingredients when it comes to curing fish.

Ingredients

2 cups (500 ml) white wine vinegar

2 tablespoons stone-ground mustard

2 teaspoons sugar

1 lemon, sliced

1 small onion, sliced

2 trout, 10 inches (25 cm) each, cleaned, with heads and tails removed

2 small bay leaves

$\frac{1}{8}$ teaspoon cayenne pepper

Preparation

1. Combine the vinegar, prepared mustard, and sugar in a small saucepan. Bring to a boil, stirring occasionally, then let the vinegar mixture cool to room temperature.

2. While the vinegar mixture cools, fill a 1-quart (1-liter) jar with the sliced lemon, onion, trout, and bay leaves, and sprinkle the cayenne pepper over the top. Pour the cooled vinegar solution over the fish and close the jar. Refrigerate for 3–4 days, and eat within 1 month. Serve with good rye crisp crackers with a touch of mustard.

MUSTARD-PICKLED TROUT

Yield: 1 pint (½ liter)

This recipe can be multiplied twenty times over, depending on how much trout you have on hand. There's no cooking, so it's a great way to handle lots of fish in the summertime.

Ingredients

1 cup (250 ml) apple cider vinegar

1 teaspoon sugar

1 teaspoon prepared horseradish

1 trout, 10-inch (25-cm), cleaned, with head and tail removed

½ yellow onion, sliced

2 tablespoons sliced carrot

5 whole peppercorns, crushed

5 whole allspice berries, crushed

Preparation

1. Combine the vinegar, sugar, and horseradish in a small saucepan. Bring to a boil, stirring occasionally, and let cool to room temperature.

2. While the vinegar mixture cools, put the trout, onion slices, carrot, and spices into a 1-pint (½-liter) jar. Pour the cooled liquid over the top. Add more vinegar if the fish is not completely covered. Seal and leave in the refrigerator 3–4 days; eat within 1 month. Serve on wheat crackers with the pickled onion for garnish.

Fly fishing at the base of a waterfall (Photo © Doug Stamm)

CHILLED TROUT WITH COCKTAIL SAUCE

Yield: 2 servings

One of my favorite things to do on a hot summer day is to wade wet in the creek behind my house. Then, when it's about time to go back to work, I keep the next small trout that hits, clean it, deposit it in my creel, and make a beeline for the kitchen. In 3 minutes, it's cooked, and by the time I'm ready for dinner, my trout is properly chilled. All fish taste better fresh, and this cocktail sauce adds just the right amount of bite.

Flies (Photo © John Barsness)

Ingredients
2 trout, 10–12 inches (25–30 cm) long each, whole
½ cup (125 ml) ketchup
2 tablespoons prepared horseradish
8 drops red pepper Tabasco sauce
½ teaspoon fresh lemon juice

Cooking
1. Rinse the trout in cold water and pat dry with paper towels. Wrap in a paper towel and microwave 60 seconds on high in a 500-watt unit, 30 seconds in a 700-watt unit. Check the inside of the trout for doneness: The meat at the top of the back will be opaque, but still moist looking. Remove the paper toweling, and cover the fish with plastic wrap. Chill.

2. To make the cocktail sauce, in a small bowl or jar combine the ketchup, horseradish, pepper sauce, and lemon juice, stir well, and serve with the fish at room temperature or chilled.

CLASSIC PAN-FRIED TROUT

Yield: 2 servings

Two secrets to good pan-frying are a fresh fish anda really hot pan of oil. Animal fat like bacon grease and lard have a relatively low smoking point and don't work as well for pan-frying as peanut and canola oils. These oils will let you turn up the heat without blackening the fish. As for the fresh fish, keep it around 10 inches (25 cm) or less, so you can fit it in the pan; six inches (15 cm) or less, and you can even eat the bones.

Rainbow trout (Photo © Doug Stamm)

Ingredients
1 trout, whole
$\frac{1}{4}$ cup (60 ml) flour
$\frac{1}{4}$ cup (60 ml) cornmeal
Peanut oil

Cooking
1. Rinse the trout, and let it drip dry. Combine the flour and cornmeal, and dredge the trout in the mixture. This not only adds flavor, but prevents water drops from getting into the hot oil.
2. Pour enough peanut oil in the skillet so it is half as deep as the fish. Heat on high until the oil smokes, then turn the heat down just enough to stop the smoking.
3. Gently place the fish in the hot oil. Cook about 1 minute to a side. The fish is done when the flesh at the thickest part flakes when you insert a fork and twist gently. Serve with lemon wedges.

Arnie's Bacon-Fried Trout Breakfast

Yield: 2 servings

Arnie Haack was a gentleman; he was also a rancher and wheat farmer in Central Montana. He owned the land around one of the prettiest trout streams I've ever known. And because he let me fish there, I always brought him trout. After I'd been fishing on his place for several years, he described to me how he cooked those fish I was providing. This is his recipe.

Ingredients
$\frac{1}{2}$ pound (250 g) bacon
1 trout, 12 inches (30 cm), freshly caught and cleaned, whole
2 slices bread
2 tablespoons butter
3 eggs
2 tablespoons chokecherry jelly

Cooking
1. In a large skillet, cook the bacon over medium heat until crispy. Remove the bacon and place on a warm platter in the oven.

2. Rinse the fish and dry with paper towels, then scrape the scales off the outside with steel wool. With the bacon grease on medium heat, carefully lay the trout in the grease and cook 4 minutes to a side, until the fish is flaky.

3. While the fish is cooking, set two slices of bread in the toaster so they are ready to go.

Melt the butter in another frying pan on medium-high heat. When the butter starts sizzling, break the eggs into the pan, break the yolks, and turn the heat as far down as it will go. With your other hand, press the toaster button down. When the toast comes up (or about 2 minutes) turn the egg over and cook another 1 minute, while you put the jelly on your toast.

4. Serve the trout, eggs, bacon, toast with chokecherry jelly, and fresh-brewed coffee, and think about the hospitality of all those gentlemen ranchers while you enjoy the best breakfast in the world.

Note: Arnie swore that scraping the scales off with steel wool kept the fish from tasting so "darn oily." But be sure to use plain steel wool not the kind with soap and polish included.

BARBECUED TROUT WITH LEMON RELISH

Yield: 2 servings

Make the lemon relish in the morning before you go fishing, and it will be ready to eat when the fish come home.

Barbecued Trout with Lemon Relish

Ingredients

1 onion, sliced thin
⅓ cup (80 ml) apple cider vinegar
⅓ cup (80 ml) water
3 tablespoons sugar
1 teaspoon dried ground mustard
¼ teaspoon ground turmeric
¼ teaspoon salt
1 lemon, thinly sliced, seeds removed
1 trout, 12 inches (30 cm), whole

Cooking

1. In a small saucepan, combine the onion, vinegar, water, sugar, mustard, turmeric, and salt. Bring to a boil, then turn down to a simmer, and cook uncovered 30 minutes, until all the liquid has been absorbed and the onions are tender.

2. Blanche the lemon slices 2 minutes in boiling water, and drain well. Add the lemon to the onion mixture, and simmer another 2–3 minutes. Serve at room temperature or chilled.

3. Start four dozen charcoal briquettes or preheat the propane barbecue or. When the briquettes are white hot or the propane unit turned down to medium high, and rest of the dinner is ready, brush a little oil on the fish and lay the fish on the grill. Cook about 5 minutes to a side. Check the inside of the fish: It should be opaque across the back but moist looking when done. Serve this fresh barbecued trout with lots of lemon relish.

CAMPFOIL TROUT DINNER

Yield: 4 servings

There's something about camping, whether it's a family weekend get-away or a hunting or fishing trip. We will—and do—eat just about anything, things we'd never think of eating at home. Liverwurst, for instance; that's what I always take on camping trips. But if you're out fishing, here's a recipe that takes little preparation, tastes good, and is a lot better for you than liverwurst. Make the marinade at home, then all you have to do is keep a fire going.

Rainbow trout (Photo © Doug Stamm)

Marinade Ingredients

1 cup (250 ml) dry white wine or extra-dry
    vermouth
4 tablespoons oil
4 tablespoons apple juice
$\frac{1}{4}$ cup (80 ml) fresh cilantro leaves
$\frac{1}{2}$ teaspoon ground cumin
$\frac{1}{8}$ teaspoon cayenne pepper
$\frac{1}{2}$ teaspoon salt
$\frac{1}{4}$ teaspoon black pepper
8 green onions, chopped
4 ounces (100 g) whole mushrooms, about
    $1\frac{1}{2}$ cups (375 ml)

Trout Dinner Ingredients

4 fresh trout, about 8–10 inches (20–25 cm)
    each, whole
6 baking potatoes, scrubbed
8 ears fresh corn
Butter or margarine
4 whole red onions, dead leaves peeled off,
    top and bottom sliced off

Preparation

1. At home, in a food processor or blender, combine the wine, oil, apple juice, cilantro, cumin, cayenne, salt, and black pepper. Process 2–3 seconds so the mixture is minced but not puréed. Pour into a plastic resealable bag, add the onions and whole mushrooms to the mixture, and keep the marinade-filled bag in the cooler.

2. At camp, if you have someone to stay and watch the fire, start one before you go fishing; otherwise wait until you're done filling your creel. Catch the trout. Clean the fish, and rinse and pat them dry inside and out with paper towels. Add the trout to the marinade-filled bag, return the bag to the cooler, and marinate for about 1 hour.

Cooking

1. Prepare the vegetables by putting a pat of butter or margarine on each potato and corn cob; trim off the top and bottom of the red onion and cut an X about $\frac{1}{4}$ inch ($\frac{1}{2}$ cm) deep in the top. Top it with a pat of butter. Wrap each vegetable individually in foil, and bury them in the coals around the fire. The vegetables will take 45–60 minutes in a good fire. Check them after 45 minutes, and roll them out of the embers when they are fork tender.

2. With the vegetables cooked, remove the fish and mushrooms from the marinade, and wrap each fish individually in foil with a quarter of the mushrooms. Seal the foil well to save the juices, and throw the packets into the embers, about 8 minutes to a side, but check one after the first 8 minutes. The fish is done when the skin peels easily, and the flesh flakes easily, but is still moist looking. To serve, peel the foil off, save it for recycling, and dig in.

Note: My friend Richard Jackson, outfitter and cowboy from East Glacier, Montana, would let those trout cook a good 45 minutes, until he got all the horses fed and watered. I'd recommend that only for those who like their trout pot-roasted. I prefer my trout barely done, but then I don't have to feed and water the horses before I can sit down to dinner.

BROILED TROUT
WITH AFRICAN-STYLE HOT SAUCE

Yield: 1 serving

Brush a little of this hot sauce on the fish before you broil it, or use as a fish dip at the table, or both. But beware—this is *hot* sauce.

Deloris River cutthroat trout (Photo © R.E. Barber)

Ingredients
1 cup (250 ml) fresh lemon juice, (about 4
   lemons)
4 cloves garlic, mashed
2 tablespoons red pepper flakes
1 teaspoon freshly ground black pepper
½ teaspoon salt
1 trout, 12 inches (30 cm) long, whole

Cooking
1. Combine the lemon juice, garlic, red and black pepper, and salt in a bowl, and stir well. Set aside, either in the refrigerator or at room temperature.

2. Preheat the broiler and broiler rack. Rinse the trout and pat it dry with paper towels. Slash with a knife across the sides of the fish three or four times, and lightly brush the top with hot sauce. When the broiler is ready, remove the rack, spray or brush lightly with oil, and replace it in the oven so the fish will be about 4 inches (10 cm) from the heat. Broil 10 minutes per 1 inch (2½ cm) of thickness, measured while the fish is on its side. Turn halfway through cooking, slash the second side, and brush the top with sauce. Serve with boiled new potatoes tossed with melted butter and minced parsley. Serve the hot sauce on the side for dipping.

POACHED TROUT WITH SHRIMP SAUCE

Yield: 2–4 servings

You can go out and buy a special pan for poaching, or you can use a covered roaster for really large fish, bending the fish to fit the curve of the pan. And since this is a moist cooking method, if the pan is not quite long enough you can remove the head without drying out the fish. The point is to just barely cover the fish with seasoned liquid, and just barely boil it. Traditionally, the cooking liquid is called a court bouillon, and it is an elegant dish.

Ingredients

1 onion, diced
1 stalk celery, diced
1 carrot, diced
$\frac{1}{4}$ cup fresh lemon juice (about 1 lemon)
2 teaspoons dried summer savory
$\frac{1}{2}$ teaspoon salt
1 teaspoon pink peppercorns (black peppercorns if you don't have pink)
1 cup (250 ml) dry white wine
1 cup (250 ml) water
4 ounces (100 g) medium-sized shrimp, raw, in the shell
1 trout, 18 inches (45 cm), whole
1 tablespoon corn starch
1 tablespoon cold water

Cooking

1. In an 18-inch-long (45-cm) poacher, combine the onion, celery, carrot, lemon juice, savory, salt, peppercorns, wine, and water. Measure the thickness of the fish: the court bouillon should just cover it. If not, add water to make the measure. Bring to a boil, cover, and simmer at low heat for 10–12 minutes. Add the shrimp and continue to simmer about 3 minutes longer. Remove the shrimp, shell and devein, and set aside. You can return the shells to the poacher for a stronger shrimp flavor.

2. Bring the poaching liquid back to a slow boil. Gently lower the trout into the poacher, and return to a slow boil. Start the timer when the water begins to boil again: cook 10 minutes for each 1 inch ($2\frac{1}{2}$ cm) of thickness at the thickest part of the fish. Keep the water just below the boiling point while cooking.

3. The fish is done when the flesh flakes but is still slightly translucent in the center. Do not leave the finished trout in the court bouillon; it will continue to cook and be quite tough. Lift the fish out of the bouillon immediately and set on a warm platter to keep warm while you make the sauce.

4. To make the sauce, measure $1\frac{1}{2}$ cups (375 ml) of strained court bouillon into a saucepan. Dissolve the corn starch in the cold water, add to the bouillon, and stir over medium-high heat. Add the shrimp, bring up to a boil, and cook a few seconds until the sauce thickens.

5. To serve, peel the skin off the fish and, with a spatula, lift the top fillet off the back bone. Remove the backbone and lift the bottom fillet off the skin. Lay each serving on a plate, then spoon the sauce over the top.

CURRIED TROUT

Yield: 4 servings

We always seem to have curry powder in our camp kitchen, and carry fruit on summer fishing excursions as a substitute for sport drinks and pop to quench our thirst. All you need then is a martini drinker and someone who can catch supper. Now, I don't have anything against macaroni and cheese and wieners, but once in a while, a curried trout is a nice change.

Ingredients

2 tablespoons oil
3 tablespoons butter or margarine
1 teaspoon curry powder
1 ½ pounds (¾ kg) trout fillets
4 tablespoons extra-dry vermouth or fish stock
2 oranges, peeled and sliced
6 cups (1 ½ liters) cooked rice

Cooking

1. In a heavy pan over medium-high heat, melt the oil and butter together and add the curry powder. Cut the fillets into individual servings and pat dry with a paper towel. When the butter starts to sizzle, gently add the fillets to the pan. Cook the fish 3–4 minutes to a side, or until golden, and opaque throughout. Remove the fillets from the pan and keep warm.

2. Pour the vermouth into the pan juices, stirring constantly until the sauce comes to a slow simmer, then add the orange slices. Return to a simmer, then pour a little sauce over each fillet. Serve with rice.

Note: While I always use real rice at home, instant is handy when cooking over a campfire.

Casting for lake trout in Alaska (Photo © Erwin and Peggy Bauer)

BAKED TROUT FILLETS IN PAPRIKA SAUCE

Yield: 4 servings

Baking is an incredibly quick way to cook trout. In fact, once you put these fish in the oven, you'll barely have time to make a salad.

Ingredients

2 shallots, finely chopped, or $\frac{1}{4}$ cup (60 ml) finely chopped sweet onion

4 tablespoons butter or margarine

4 tablespoons flour

1 cup (250 ml) fish stock, leftover court or chicken bouillon

$\frac{1}{2}$ cup (125 ml) white wine

$\frac{1}{4}$ cup (60 ml) table cream, or $\frac{1}{4}$ cup (60 ml) whipping cream plus $\frac{1}{4}$ cup (60ml) 1 percent milk

1 teaspoon sweet Hungarian paprika

$1\frac{1}{2}$ pounds ($\frac{3}{4}$ kg) trout fillets

4 large tomatoes, sliced

Cooking

1. In a saucepan, sauté the shallots in the butter until softened and add the flour. Cook on medium heat, stirring constantly until the flour is well mixed. Stir in the stock and wine, and continue stirring until all the sauce is smooth. Add the table cream and paprika, stir until well mixed, and simmer about 1 more minute. Remove from the heat.

2. Preheat the oven to 400°F (205°C). In a lightly buttered baking dish, layer the fillets and tomato slices, and pour the sauce over the top. Bake, uncovered, about 10 minutes per 1 inch ($2\frac{1}{2}$ cm) of thickness, or until the fillets are opaque throughout but still moist.

SMOKED TROUT

Yield: 1 trout

Here's one of those treats that's always welcome at a party. Or make it just for yourself. It stores well, as long as 1 month in your refrigerator, 3 months in the freezer, and is a healthy between-meal treat.

Smoked Trout

Ingredients
1 quart (1 liter) hot water
½ cup (125 ml) sugar
½ cup (125 ml) salt
1 teaspoon black peppercorns
1 teaspoon granulated lemon peel
1 trout, 14 inches (35 cm) long, whole

Preparation
1. Combine all the ingredients except the trout in a 1-quart (1-liter) canning jar. Mix until the salt and sugar are dissolved, then let the brine cool to room temperature.
2. In the meantime, rinse the fish, and pat dry with a paper towel. Place it in a non-corrosive dish small enough to hold the fish completely submerged in the brine. When the brine has cooled, pour it over the fish, cover with plastic wrap, and refrigerate 12 hours, turning occasionally. Since fish have a tendency to float, you may have to weigh it down with a saucer to keep it submerged.
3. Remove the fish from the brine, rinse gently, and pat dry with paper towels. Allow to air dry at room temperature for 1–2 hours until the flesh is slightly sticky. The fish is now ready for the smoker.

Smoking

1. For an electric smoker, soak your wood chips in the smoking pan for 30 minutes, then drain off the excess liquid before using. Place the chip pan in the smoker, turn the smoker on, and wait 15 minutes, or until the first sign of smoke appears: in other words, preheat the smoker. When the smoker is ready, place the fish on a shelf as far from the heat as possible, or hang it from a hook. Prop open the body cavity with a couple of toothpicks. For moderate smoke flavor, refill the chip pan two more times during the smoking.,

2. Cook until the flesh is opaque throughout, 8–10 hours at 140–150°F (60–65°C). Ambient air temperature plays a role; on a 55°F-degree (13°C) day, it takes exactly 9 hours in my smoker at the temperatures listed above. Colder days will take longer, warmer days, less time.

3. Serve immediately with mustard, cream cheese, or a slice of apple on a cracker, or store for later. See general directions for smoking on page 96 for details on wood and storage.

Note: Save your brine solution and reuse it up to two more times. You can double or triple the recipe and make as many trout as will fit loosely in the smoker.

Trout fishing at dawn in Jordan Lake in the Beartooth Mountains of Montana (Photo © Erwin and Peggy Bauer)

SMOKED TROUT SALAD WITH RASPBERRY VINEGAR DRESSING

Yield: 2–4 servings

So you made enough smoked trout for the next ten years, and you're having trouble thinking up enough parties to serve it at? Try a rich, tangy salad. It's filling enough for winter, but cool enough for summer. And don't get put off by that raspberry vinegar: it's not fruity. It's a rich-tasting, hearty accompaniment for the strong flavor of smoked trout.

Smoked Trout Salad with Raspberry Vinegar Dressing

Dressing Ingredients

¼ cup (60 ml) raspberry vinegar
¼ cup (60 ml) oil
1 tablespoon Dijon mustard
2 teaspoons fresh lemon juice
2 teaspoons honey
½ teaspoon black pepper
4 tablespoons buttermilk or non-fat yogurt (optional)

Salad Ingredients

½ head romaine lettuce
1 smoked trout, 15 inches (37½ cm) long
1 red Delicious apple, cored and diced
1 cup (250 ml) coarsely chopped, unsalted walnuts
3 ripe plum or roma tomatoes, diced
1 red bell pepper, sliced

Preparation

1. Combine all the dressing ingredients in a glass jar. Shake well. Chill until ready to serve and shake well at serving time.
2. Tear the lettuce off the head and use it to line four bowls. Remove the flesh from the skin and bones of the trout and flake coarsely into a large bowl. Add the diced apple, chopped walnuts, diced tomatoes, and red pepper. Toss and divide between the four plates of lettuce. Drizzle 1–2 tablespoons of dressing over each salad and serve.

SPRING CREEK SPAGHETTI

Yield: 4–6 servings

This looks like a traditional spaghetti sauce, but instead of red meat, it has trout. Find a spring creek that's open to fly fishing all winter, and catch the trout fresh for dinner. Make it a tradition at least once a winter to fish with your gloves on.

Ingredients

½ medium yellow onion, chopped

3 cloves garlic, minced

2 tablespoons oil

1 tablespoon dried parsley flakes

1 tablespoon dried leaf basil

1 teaspoon dried rosemary, crushed

1 teaspoon dried leaf sage

12 ounces (300 g) trout meat, diced or shredded

1 cup (125 ml) dry white wine

1 can whole tomatoes, 28 ounces (795 g), diced

½ teaspoon salt

¼ teaspoon pepper

1 pound (½ kg) spaghetti, cooked

½ cup (125 ml) grated Parmesan cheese

Cooking

1. In a medium saucepan over medium heat, sauté the onion and garlic in the oil until slightly browned, about 5 minutes. Add the parsley, basil, rosemary, and sage, and cook another 1–2 minutes. Add the trout to the seasoned onion, stir, and cook for about 5 minutes. Raise the heat to high, add the wine, and cook until almost all the excess liquid is gone. While the wine cooks down, start a large pot of water and cook the spaghetti *al dente*.

2. Reduce the heat under the trout to medium, add the tomatoes, salt, and pepper, and cook another 5 minutes. Drain the spaghetti and serve with the trout sauce topped with Parmesan cheese.

THE BARD OF TROUT CREEK

Yield: 4 servings

Barding is an ancient method of adding fat—and flavor—to meat. Wrapping these delicate little trout with bacon also adds a smoky taste to the freshest food around.

Ingredients

4 trout, 10–12 inches (25–30 cm) long each, whole
1 tablespoon white wine vinegar
1 teaspoon salt
1 tablespoon vegetable oil
8 slices lean bacon

Cooking

1. Preheat the broiler and broiler pan, or propane barbecue, or start 3 dozen charcoal briquettes, or start a campfire. Set a propane barbecue to medium high for cooking; for the charcoal briquettes and campfires, the fire is ready when you can't hold your hand 4–6 inches (10–15 cm) over the coals for more than 2–3 seconds. Set the grill at that level. If you use a hinged grate to hold the fish, preheat that, too.
2. Rinse the fish and pat dry with paper towels. Sprinkle a little of the vinegar and salt inside each one, then rub lightly with oil inside and out. Remove and lightly oil the preheated grill or broiler rack you will be cooking on. If you use a hinged grate be sure to oil that, too. Do not spray oil directly over the fire. The grill, grate, or broiler rack should be hot enough to mark the fish.
3. While the broiler, barbecue, or fire heats up, fry the bacon in a skillet on medium heat until lightly browned to render part of the fat. Wrap each fish in 2 slices of bacon and secure with toothpicks, if necessary. Lay the trout on the broiler rack or grill and cook about 10 minutes per 1 inch (2½ cm) of thickness. The fish is done when the flesh inside is opaque through to the spine. Serve with potato salad and green beans fresh from the garden or farmer's market.

Early morning trout fishing in Flathead Lake, Montana (Photo © Erwin and Peggy Bauer)

SCRAMBLED ROE

Yield: 2 servings

Since we generally fish catch-and-release during the spawn, we consider trout roe a rarity. Sauté it gently in butter alongside the trout, or make this delicious fortified egg dish. With cinnamon roll and coffee, it might just be the most nutritionally complete breakfast for anglers.

Ingredients

$\frac{1}{2}$ cup (125 ml) roe, or less if that's all you have
4 large eggs
3 tablespoons milk
$\frac{1}{2}$ teaspoon salt
$\frac{1}{4}$ teaspoon black pepper, or $\frac{1}{8}$ teaspoon cayenne
2 tablespoons butter

Preparation

If you are planning to keep a fish during the spawn, bring a resealable plastic bag with you to keep the roe clean. To remove the roe, turn the fish upside down—vent to the sky—open the belly, and scoop the roe into the bag with one clean hand while you hold the fish with the other. Put the roe on ice until you get home, then immediately rinse them gently in cool tap water in a colander or sieve. Cook that night. If you want to wait for the next day's breakfast, return them to the rinsed bag and refrigerate.

Cooking

1. Break the chicken eggs into a bowl, and add the milk, salt, pepper, and trout roe. Beat lightly with a fork. Melt the butter in a large skillet, over medium-high heat until the butter is hot but not sizzling. Pour the egg mixture into the pan and lower the heat to medium.

2. As soon as the eggs start to solidify, begin stirring gently with a fork or spoon, moving the eggs away from the sides of the pan into the center. When the eggs are still soft and shiny but not runny, transfer immediately to a plate.

3. Serve with cinnamon rolls and fresh-brewed coffee. If you are lucky enough to be traveling through Dillon, Montana, stop at Anna's Oven for the lightest, most delicious cinnamon rolls you'll ever eat.

ROCKY MOUNTAIN SUSHI

Yield: 8–10 servings

I'm sharing this recipe with you on the condition that you make it exactly as I say. Never, never, never eat raw fish unless you freeze it first at 0°F (−17.8°C) for at least 48–72 hours. Use a freezer thermometer to be sure. Any fish that appears in this cookbook lives in waters where parasites live. Cooking and freezing destroy them. That said, sushi is a delicious way to eat trout and salmon, and I thank Seiji, Masa, and Keizo, three gentlemen from Tokyo, Japan, for introducing me to it.

Rocky Mountain Sushi

Ingredients

1 trout, whole, 16 inches (40 cm) long or just large enough to fillet

3 cups (750 ml) cooked Japanese rice, or white rice, cooked very sticky, room temperature

2 teaspoons white rice vinegar

2 teaspoons hot Chinese mustard

Preparation

1. Catch, clean, and freeze the trout at 0°F (−17.8°C) for 48–72 hours. Thaw in the refrigerator overnight. Thawing on the counter will allow bacteria to grow.

2. Just before you are ready to serve, fillet the fish, removing the skin as well. Cut the fillet in half lengthwise. Cut across the two halves with a sharp knife, cutting pieces about ½ inch (1 cm) thick. Set aside.

3. Put the cooked, cooled rice in a bowl, sprinkle with the vinegar, and toss with your hands. Then, shape the rice into cylinders, about 2 inches (5 cm) in diameter, and 3–4 inches (7.5–10 cm) in length.

4. Lay the raw fish over the rice cylinders, dot with the hot Chinese mustard, and serve as an appetizer.

TERIYAKI CUTBOW

Yield: just enough

Masa Watanabe is a sporting-goods dealer in Tokyo, and doesn't fish. So while Judy, Cindy, and I fly-fished for the delicious cross-bred, cutthroat-rainbow trout near Glacier Park in Montana, Masa collected firewood and started a fire. It was a hot afternoon, and at first we thought building a fire an odd pasttime. Then we caught a fish. "Teriyaki," he said, his only English, and disappeared with our catch. In ten minutes, Masa returned with our cutbow, delicately roasted on a stick. It was one of the best trout I've ever eaten.

Ingredients

1 trout, under 12 inches (30 cm) long, whole but not cleaned

Preparation

1. Start a fire on the bank, in about a 2-foot (60-cm) ring, while everyone else rigs up. Dry driftwood works best for the fuel—but no evergreen. Peel a live willow branch for the cooking stick.

2. Wait for your friends to catch a fish. (I think I might like this part, at least once in a while. It might be fun to keep asking if anyone's caught anything yet.)

3. Once you have a fish, kill it, but *do not clean it*. Having the fish whole helps keep it on the willow stick. Run the willow stick into the mouth, and firmly into the viscera. Don't run it out through the tail.

Cooking

1. Gently, but quickly, sear the outside of the fish—without blackening—by holding it about 4–6 inches (10–15 cm) above the highest flames.

2. Once the outside is seared, prop the stick up on a rock, keeping the fish within the circle of heat, but not directly in contact with the fire. About 10 minutes will do for an 8-inch (20-cm) fish, 1–2 minutes longer for a larger trout. The fish is done when the skin peels away easily and the flesh on either side of the spine is flaky but moist.

3. To serve, leave the fish on the stick. Find your fishing friends, and let them pick the meat off the bones, until it is gone, and you have another fish to cook. Masa cooked up 4 trout before we made him stop, and they were all delicious.

INDEX

ABOUT THE AUTHOR

Eileen Clarke combines her three loves in this cookbook: fishing, writing, and experimenting with food. She is also the author of *The Art of Wild Game Cooking*, which includes recipes for big game, small game, birds, and fish, and *The Venison Cookbook*. Her many articles on hunting, conservation, and natural history have appeared in numerous magazines, including *Field & Stream*, *Gray's Sporting Journal*, *Wyoming Wildlife*, *Shooting Sportsman*, and *Montana Outdoors*. She won first place prizes for her articles from the Outdoor Writer's Association of America in 1993 and 1995. Her first novel, *The Queen of the Legal Tender Saloon*, will be published next year. In the meantime, she's applying for moose, sheep, and antelope permits, tuning up her bow, stringing her new six-foot fly rod, and going bear hunting.

Eileen Clarke at work (Photo © John Barsness)